Integrating the Literature of Roald Dahl in the Classroom

by
Thomas J. Palumbo

illustrated by Judy Hierstein

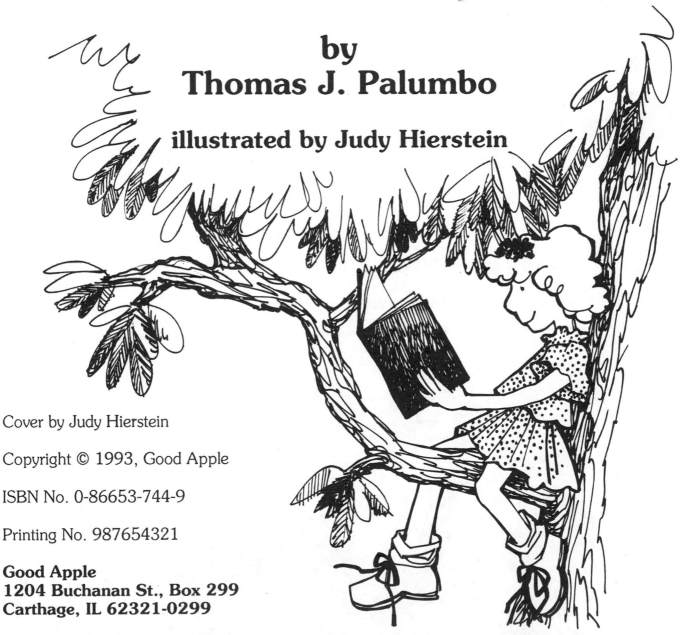

Cover by Judy Hierstein

Copyright © 1993, Good Apple

ISBN No. 0-86653-744-9

Printing No. 987654321

Good Apple
1204 Buchanan St., Box 299
Carthage, IL 62321-0299

A Paramount Communications Company

Table of Contents

Introducing Roald Dahl

"The Wheel Is Made for You . . . Why Reinvent It?"

Integrating the Literature of Roald Dahl in the Classroom is the fifth book in a series focusing on the most read authors in contemporary children's literature. Like its four predecessors, *Integrating the Literature of Judy Blume in the Classroom, Integrating the Literature of Beverly Cleary in the Classroom, Integrating the Literature of Chris Van Allsburg in the Classroom* and *Integrating the Literature of Maurice Sendak in the Classroom*, this book uses fourteen steps necessary for developing and maximizing the educational benefits of literature used in the classroom or home. These steps include Book Cover Introduction (motivational discussion/art), Lead-Ins to Literature (children starters/critical thinking), Just the Facts (comprehension skills), What Is Your Opinion? (creative analysis of ideas/opinions), Vexing Vocabulary (word development and use), Drills for Skills (challenging tasks, games and puzzles), Ideas and Illustrations (art projects), Short-Term Projects (children becoming idea producers), Student Suggestions (integrating literature), Teacher Suggestions (classroom extenders), Write Like a Master (formats for writing like a master), Public Speaking (speech topics), Follow-Up Games (multilevel gameboards), Bulletin Boards That Teach (teacher/student-made displays).

Everything is completed for the classroom teacher or book enthusiast. The steps are multilevel and can be read to or by children when doing each activity. The activities lend themselves to teacher and student input. Each idea conforms to fit educational goals, classroom literature objectives and student learning styles. After combining the ideas in this guide with your own ideas and your curriculum guides format, you'll find that there are very few gaps in your literature and language arts program.

GA1459

Author's Notes

After completing books on Beverly Cleary, Judy Blume, Chris Van Allsburg and Maurice Sendak, I thought I would have a hard time finding another author to focus on that

1. Has written at least ten books
2. Is universally recognized for a variety of literary topics
3. Would appeal to the reading tastes of my students
4. Correlates to our standard literature curriculum
5. Excites/Challenges the classroom teacher's creativity

My niece, Allesan Palumbo, age 5, gave me the answer. While watching *Charlie and the Chocolate Factory* with her for the one hundredth time, I asked her why. She said it was funny. When you reach your twenty-sixth year of teaching, you'll realize if it is funny to children, literary knowledge can be developed and extended. Every time I try to say something important in my books, it comes out hollow. Up until that point, for some unknown reason, I never used Roald Dahl in the classroom . . . so, it was off to the library. *The Wonderful Story of Henry Sugar and Six More*, my first Dahl adventure, immediately won me over. Please, don't tell my students that my selection was based on the book's hard cover. It will kill my lessons on the "right way" to select a book. Nonetheless, the book looked more professional than some of the paperback versions that were previewed. The seven stories had something in them for everyone.

Everything a multigrade teacher might stress in creative writing was there: challenging and imaginative stories, dialogue developers, autobiographical sketches and diverse themes. In the weeks that followed, more time was spent reading than giving tests. Maybe my students just conned me into thinking they wanted to hear more.

The professional quality of independent work and short-term projects using the Dahl books served as excellent student involvement indicators. Teeth didn't have to be pulled to make classes research "Famous Giants of Fact or Fiction" (*The BFG*) or to survey literature concerning "the intelligence" of animals (*The Boy Who Could Talk with Animals*). Children were discussing and suggesting other Dahl books to their classmates without any prompting from the teacher.

It is my hope that using this Dahl guide and the other four guides in this series will develop in your students a greater love and appreciation of an author's body of work and save teachers hours of preplanning.

The BFG

Human Bean

Queen Elizabeth

Mr. Tibbs

Fleshlumpeater

Funny Speech

Sophie's Giant Watching

Frobscottle **Dream Bottles**

1

GA1459

Lead-Ins to Literature

I don't want to bring up bad experiences. However, I am interested in your worst nightmares. Being carried away by a giant was always my worst nightmare. It was so bad that my mother had to take me to the doctor. The doctor said I had "Jack and the Beanstalk" phobia. If you believe that outrageous story, you'll love *The BFG*. Sophie, one of the lead characters in the story, is carried from her bed in the middle of the night. The person doing the carrying is a ten-foot giant. The strange saga of Sophie, England and Giantsville is chronicled in *The BFG*. Hold tight while your teacher reads the story to you.

1. If you were to be snatched by a giant, would you rather be snatched by a young or an old giant? Why? Present your reasons why both ages might treat you well or poorly. _____
   _____
   _____

2. What three reasons might a giant have for snatching young children?
   a. _____
   b. _____
   c. _____

3. Would you stage this story in modern times? Don't you think it would be a little more believable if it were in olden days? _____
   _____
   _____

4. Before reading the story, write down five features that you think the author will give his giant. After reading the story, see how many of your features match the author's. Then on the back of this paper, make a mini drawing of a giant. Give your giant three features that would make it head and heels above all the rest of the giants in children's stories.
   a. _____
   b. _____
   c. _____
   d. _____
   e. _____

5. What or who is your favorite monster from children's stories? Why? _____
   _____
   _____

6. Would you expect boys and girls to act the same when being snatched by a giant? _____
   _____
   _____

7. If you were a giant that acted like the tooth fairy and left something each time you snatched a child, what three things would you leave? _____
   _____
   _____

GA1459

Just the Facts

1. The first question is, of course, the hardest one to answer. What does *BFG* mean? _____

    _____

2. In what kind of room did Sophie sleep? _____

3. All the people were in a deep, deep sleep, and all the dark things came out at what time of

    night? _____

4. What did the head of the air force fly off in the Atlas? _____

5. What was the BFG's only food source? _____

6. What use did the BFG have for a trumpet? _____

7. Name five things that the BFG said incorrectly. _____

    _____

8. Sophie found that the book _____ was used by the BFG to teach himself to read.

9. The BFG used what wind as an example of something that survives without anyone feeding

    it? _____

10. The queen's maid almost fainted when she saw Sophie on the window ledge. What phrase

    was used to describe her appearance? _____

11. The BFG had unusual ears and he requested that they not be _____ at.

12. Dead trees were everywhere near the giant's cave. What color were the rocks that were

    found in the area? _____

13. The worst of the bad dreams were three things in one. What three words did the BFG use to

    describe the bad nightmares? _____ _____ _____

14. The queen had to check Sophie's and the giant's story about missing people. What two

    rulers did she call to verify their stories? _____ _____

Write five questions of your own from one of the chapters. Exchange questions with a classmate before he or she reads that chapter. Each of you should jot the correct answer down on a piece of paper when you get to that part of the story.

a. _____

b. _____

c. _____

d. _____

e. _____

GA1459

What Is Your Opinion?

1. There are a great many legends from Bigfoot to the Loch Ness Monster to the Yeti Snowman that remain in people's minds. Do you think it is possible that a giant could possibly live in the twentieth century and still remain hidden? _____

_____

_____

_____

2. What would you think of a dream store where you could take a dream of your own home for the night just like you would rent a video? _____

_____

_____

_____

3. Did you believe the part of the story about dreams being lonesome? _____

_____

_____

_____

4. The BFG ate only one type of food. Could you possibly survive on only one food? Mine would be broccoli and meatball pizza with red sauce. What would yours be? _____

_____

_____

_____

5. The BFG read Shakespeare and Dickens, two excellent writers. Do you think reading good writers helps you to become a better writer? _____

_____

_____

_____

6. Orphanages always get a bad reputation in children's stories. Do you think they deserve all the negative things people say about them? Please explain. _____

_____

_____

_____

7. Why do you think Sophie would make a good friend to anyone in the community who might be a little different or who has some major problems? _____

_____

_____

_____

8. On the back of this sheet, write a critique of the book *The BFG*. Make believe you're Siskel and get someone to critique who would represent Ebert, the movie commentators.

GA1459

Giant Word Switches
Vexing Vocabulary

The BFG switches all kinds of words around. He has a terrible time with vocabulary. Sophie, nevertheless, seems to understand what he is saying throughout the whole story. Ten of his giant switches are described below. To make it easier for you, the page number has also been given. Place what the giant really means beside what he originally said in the spaces provided. Then rewrite the sentence with its proper phrasing under each. Try some comparable switches of your own in the five spaces provided at the bottom of the page.

Giant Switches   **Your Switches**

1. Little ants chittering–page 44 _____little ants chattering_____
   I heard the little ants chattering as they scampered around the floor.

2. Dropping buzzbombs–page 132 _____
   _____

3. Emptier than a bundongle–page 26_____
   _____

4. Rack Jobinson–page 201 _____
   _____

5. Majester/Monacher–page 159_____
   _____

6. Squackling good idea–page 131 _____
   _____

7. Filthsome–page 67_____
   _____

8. Throte–page 105 _____
   _____

9. Kitshun–page 104 _____
   _____

10. Rotrasper–page 39 _____
    _____

11. _____
12. _____
13. _____
14. _____
15. _____

GA1459

Fleshlumpeater Words
Drills for Skills

Each clue will generate a word dedicated to the *ump* in Fleshlumpeater's name. Examine the clue. After finding the answer to the clue, place the number of vowels over the total number of letters in the word to find your fraction.

Clue	Answer	Fraction
This *ump* can be found		
Example: on a person's head	bump	$^1/_4$
1. after a tree is cut		
2. in baseball		
3. pulled out grass		
4. musical instrument		
5. trash spot		
6. a dwarf		
7. camel part		
8. a childhood disease		
9. English for "a pal"		
10. a child's name		
11. type of beans		
12. flat fixer		
13. thunder sound		
14. baby stealer in fairy tales		
15. turkey describer		

Place five of your clues for *ump*, *imp* or *amp* words below. Challenge classmates with their solution.

1. _____
2. _____
3. _____
4. _____
5. _____

Character Building
Short-Term Project

Most authors sketch a descriptive outline of each of their characters before starting a story. The outline helps them to define the appearance and direction that their lead and minor characters might take. You are building a monster. On the left write the features of each of your monster's body parts. Three boxes appear on the right for your three best drawings of individual body parts.

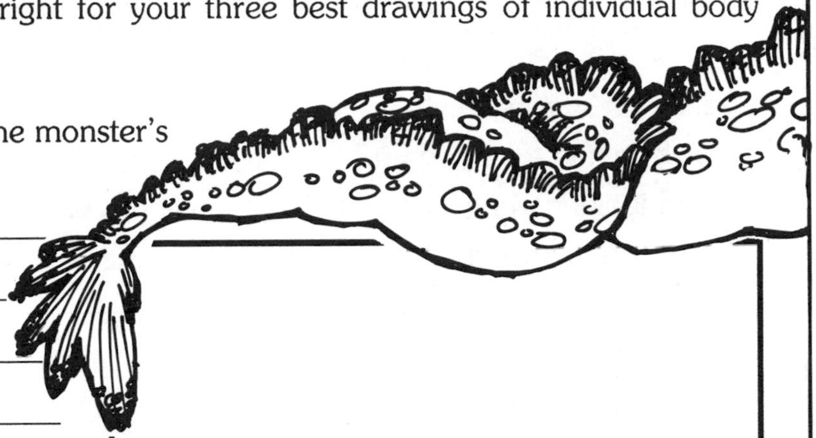

Here are my notes for the description of the monster's parts.

Hands _____

_____

_____

Face _____

_____

_____

Feet _____

_____

_____

Body _____

_____

_____

Odor _____

_____

_____

Childhood _____

_____

_____

Mind/Brain _____

_____

_____

Write a description of your monster on the back of this paper. Your monster could be likeable like the one in *The BFG* or *The Reluctant Dragon*.

GA1459

Ideas and Illustrations

Below are seven ideas suggested for the cover of *The BFG*. Add five illustration ideas that you might suggest after you complete the story. Choose two illustration suggestions from the original seven below, and show how you would have completed the cover for this story. Notice how four or five ideas from each story have been put on the cover page. This is called the "collage technique." Try this technique with some of your other school topics. Use two large pieces of paper for your artwork and make two brief sketches below for your teacher's approval.

Illustration suggestions:

1. Two giants scooping up children
2. Girl looking out window at giants running down street
3. Three jars on a shelf with dream labels on them
4. Giant walking over the palace walls
5. Giant and young girl bowing to the queen
6. Tanks attacking giants
7. Orphanage closed sign/children missing

Your suggestions, if you were the author of this activity book:

1. _____
2. _____
3. _____
4. _____
5. _____

Your two drawings:

GA1459

Student Suggestions

1. Review our Declaration of Independence and Bill of Rights. Then see if you can find a copy of the English Bill of Rights/Magna Carta. Using these three documents as a foundation, create a giant's bill of rights. Try to put in five serious points and five humorous ones. Mentally place yourself in the body of a giant. What would you expect in the form of common courtesies and behavior from those around you? Some of my students wrote the ideas from the Bill of Rights and under them changed the wording to reflect the desires of a person who might be a giant.

2. Review the film/story *Ben and Me*. Write a humorous short story titled "Fleshlumpeater and Me." Focus on your ability to change a hideous character into someone who could gain respect from all those around him.

3. You are the owner of a special needs furniture store. Create a portfolio of furniture fit for a giant. Divide your portfolio into three sections. The sections could include children's, adult's and space-age furniture for giants. If you don't like furniture, how about a clothing or toys-for-giants portfolio?

4. Design a video game that would feature the BFG, Fleshlumpeater and Sophie.

5. Make a flip book highlighting the friendship of Sophie and the BFG.

6. Make believe you are Robin Leach of the television show *Lifestyles of the Rich and Famous*. Take your classmates on a tour of England, London, or Buckingham Palace. Conduct an interview with Queen Elizabeth, Princess Diana or one of the children. You're the interviewer and one of your classmates is the Queen or Princess.

7. Create a menu that would attract giants to your restaurant. Have foods named after characters in *The BFG*. You could feature Fleshlumpeater Eggs, Sophie Soda or BFG Goose. Be sure to include the special ingredients that would relate to the character the food characterizes.

8. There are very few female giants or monsters in children's books. Draw and create a giant female character that would assist Sophie and the BFG.

9. Roald Dahl served in the Royal Air Force. Research the RAF's history and make a mini poster asking people to join the RAF. Feature some of the RAF's aircraft and special history, especially in World War II. Find out as much as you can about Americans in the RAF before World War II.

10. Make a poster titled "The Best of Big Ben and London Bridge." Have your poster feature five events in English history through the eyes of the clock and the bridge.

Teacher Suggestions

1. Play Wheel of Fortune with your class using terms from English history. Vocabulary might include Windsor Castle, Thames River, White Cliffs of Dover, Buckingham Palace, Yorkshire pudding, The Tower of London, Sherlock Holmes, House of Lords, Oxford University and a host of others. The scoring system gives twenty-five points to the team that gets the answer and additional points for vowels (5) and consonants (10) that were not revealed when the particular team guessed the right answer. Twenty-five points are also given for explaining the significance of the correct answer.

2. Have a king or queen for a day presentation with students appearing as kings and queens from English history. Everyone in the class wanted to be Henry the Eighth. We put names in a hat and selected one girl and one boy for Henry. I was happy with the student selections of monarchs that weren't as well-known as Henry.

3. Discuss with your class the positive and negative aspects of being a giant.

4. Have your students create and illustrate dream jars. This activity was outstanding. I gave each student a giant pickle jar cutout to trace. Seven picked shapes of their own. Then they put dream drawings on their jars with a 3" x 5" (7.62 x 12.7 cm) card under each to describe the happening. Four mini scenes from their dreams had to be incorporated on each jar. One jar contained good dreams, hopes and wishes. The second jar could contain a nightmare. I encouraged good dreams in both, but you know children!

5. Explain what a storyboard is to your children. It is often called the writer's flowchart. Have your kids create storyboards for the sequel to *The BFG*.

6. Have your class create a commercial with one of the characters from *The BFG* and a famous athlete or movie star. Explain the blue screen technique to them of filming stars in front of a blue screen and then later creating a scene behind them. Ask them to record five scenes from movies or television where they think this technique is employed.

7. Using the *Guinness Book of World Records*, have your children create bar graphs showing average height compared to the tallest human on record, average portion of spaghetti to the most consumed in an hour, fastest car to the average allowed speed, longest time awake to the average time awake.

8. Have your class write as a giant seeking employment. Discuss the jobs a giant might excel in doing.

GA1459

Write Like a Master

The theme for each story starter below is that of placing a giant in an ordinary situation. Of course, it is ordinary for us but not someone who is twelve feet (3.65 m) tall. Make your writing serious, humorous and understanding of the plight of someone that tall.

Story Starter I

How does Mrs. Robinson expect us to put a giant on our bowling team? His fingers take up half the ball. Why doesn't he play basketball or football? I know she says he doesn't like those sports, but it isn't fair that _____

_____

_____

_____

Story Starter II

Fast food drive-up window dialogue: Car driver: I'd like to order twenty cheeseburgers, twenty large fries and fifteen milk shakes. Window clerk: That's quite an order. What do you have, a giant in the car with you? Car driver: As a matter of fact _____

_____

_____

_____

Story Starter III

Look, Fleshlumpeater! I don't care how big your father is. If you don't finish writing, "I will not snort in class 1000 times," I! I! Oh! Hello, Mr. Extrafleshlumpeater. Fleshy isn't having a good day. He _____

_____

_____

_____

Story Starter IV

It isn't easy being a giant, especially a friendly one. You don't have any friends. People read all those weird science fiction books and think all giants have to_____

_____

_____

_____

Story Starter V

Finish this poem. Go for twelve lines in abab form.

Sally is the friendliest of giants
Special in hundreds of ways;
She is kind, considerate and gentle
And a fan of musical plays.

GA1459

Public Speaking

Public speaking is the newest teaching component in this literature series. You are responsible for a one-minute speech on any one of the topics listed below. There is a space after each topic for brief notes. This will give your teacher an opportunity to see that you are headed in the right direction before actually giving your speech.

1. You are explaining to the queen reasons why she shouldn't be frightened when she sees the BFG.

   _____

   _____

   _____

2. You are giving a speech in the English House of Commons/Lords describing the necessity for attacking the nine giants.

   _____

   _____

   _____

3. You are the teacher of a horrible class of giants. What points will your first speech to them about your classroom contain? Rules of behavior/topics of study?

   _____

   _____

   _____

4. You are an orphan who is meeting possible parents. What will you say to them when they ask you to tell about yourself? Do this speech as an imaginary person, not yourself.

   _____

   _____

   _____

5. You are the commander of an army of giants who must give your giants strategies to avoid being detected in their travels and people stealing. How would you direct your faithful men and women?

   _____

   _____

   _____

6. You are giving a speech to raise money for your local zoo or art museum. Your city wants to close or lessen the visiting hours to save money in its budget.

   _____

   _____

   _____

Place three of your own speech topics on the back of this sheet. Please check with your teacher for approval.

12

Gameboard

Materials Needed: Two number cubes, movers, light-colored crayons; Vexing Vocabulary; Just the Facts. Student-made and teacher-made question cards can be placed around the gameboard. They are optional but highly recommended. A card is picked each time a player has a multiple of ten points in his or her bank. Players earn five points for each word recorded.

Players Needed: Two to four players or teams of two players

Play Procedures: Players alternate turns; throw number cubes; move in either direction at any time. This allows for playing strategies, rather than just mindlessly moving around a gameboard.

The Roll: Roll both number cubes. Your teacher will tell you to conduct some math operations with the number cubes. The three rules used most often in my classroom are

    a. Subtract the smaller from the larger; then move that many spaces (6 - 4 = $\underline{2}$. Move two spaces.)

    b. Multiply the two cubes and move the number of spaces in the one's column of the answer (2 x 6 = 1$\underline{2}$. Move two spaces.)

    c. Keep on adding the two cubes until you get one digit as the answer (6 + 6 = 12, 12 = 1 + 2 = $\underline{3}$. Move three spaces.) Mathematicians call this finding the digital root.

Object: To score thirty-five points or to capture a box of four squares in the middle of the gameboard. This can be accomplished by landing on a word box in a normal turn, trading for word boxes when you land on a trading post or buying *one* of them for two times its value when you land on the bank. Each time you land on a word piece, you try to combine it with a piece in the middle to make a word. You can use the blank gameboard to create your own variations. Record your words in the bank below. Ownership will change after trades only. Cross them out on the score sheet and add them to the other column. A scoreboard is provided for you.

Winning: Words will vary. The game is designed so two or three words can be made from each landing area.

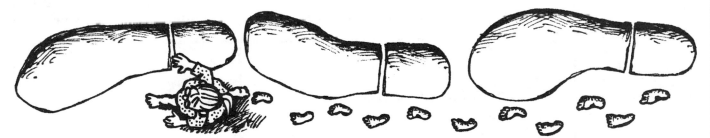

Player One's Words/Score	Player Two's Words/Score
Word Bank	**Word Bank**
1. _____	1. _____
2. _____	2. _____
3. _____	3. _____
4. _____	4. _____
5. _____	5. _____

GA1459

The BFG
Drawing Work Sheet I
Ideas and Illustrations

The author likes playing this game as an art activity. In this version you are trying to make words that appear on the drawing work sheet. Six pictures are already given to you. You must also make six predictions of words that you will be forming when the game starts. If you capture that word, you enter it in your word bank and reproduce the illustrator's drawing. If you make a word that you predicted you'd land on, then you and your opponent draw that picture in the space provided.

Player One's Words/Score	Player Two's Words/Score

Word	Illustrator's Drawing	Student's Copy	Student's Prediction	Player 1's Drawing	Player 2's Drawing
cow					
jar			rat		
well					
pan			pill		
tar					
van					

GA1459

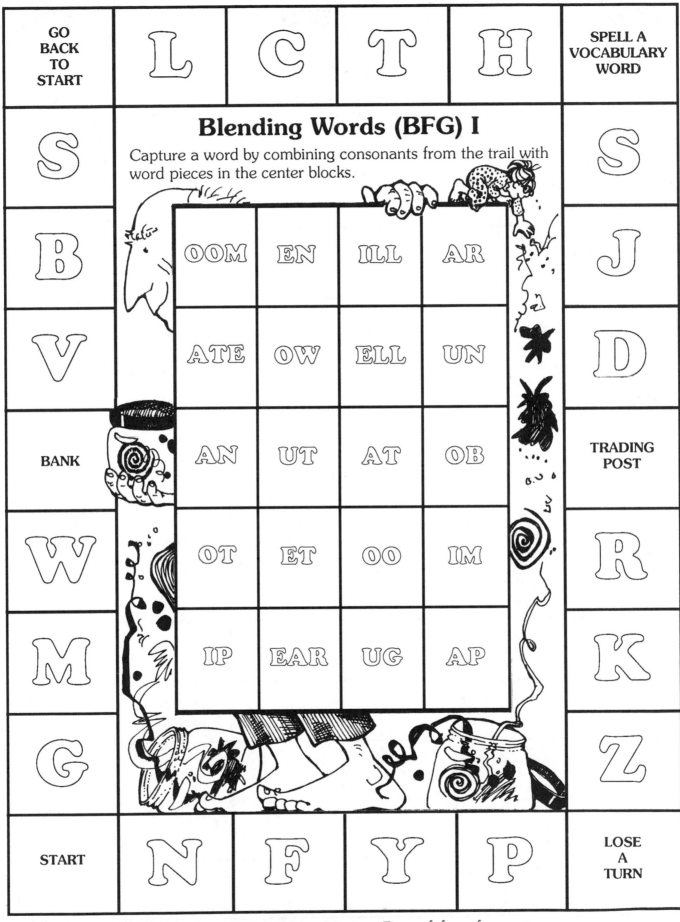

Blending Words (BFG) I

Capture a word by combining consonants from the trail with word pieces in the center blocks.

OOM	EN	ILL	AR
ATE	OW	ELL	UN
AN	UT	AT	OB
OT	ET	OO	IM
IP	EAR	UG	AP

Trail letters (outer board):

GO BACK TO START · L · C · T · H · SPELL A VOCABULARY WORD

S · S

B · J

V · D

BANK · TRADING POST

W · R

M · K

G · Z

START · N · F · Y · P · LOSE A TURN

Three boxes in a row is a winner. Box of four for upper grades.

GA1459

The BFG
Drawing Work Sheet II
Ideas and Illustrations

The author likes playing this game as an art activity. In this version you are trying to make words that appear on the drawing work sheet. Six pictures are already given to you. You must also make six predictions of words that you will be forming when the game starts. If you capture that word, you enter it in your word bank and reproduce the illustrator's drawing. If you make a word that you predicted you'd land on, then you and your opponent draw that picture in the space provided.

Player One's Words/Score	Player Two's Words/Score

Word	Illustrator's Drawing	Student's Copy	Student's Prediction	Player 1's Drawing	Player 2's Drawing
chess (piece)					
trout					
store			ship		
dream					
thread			troll		
grill					

GA1459

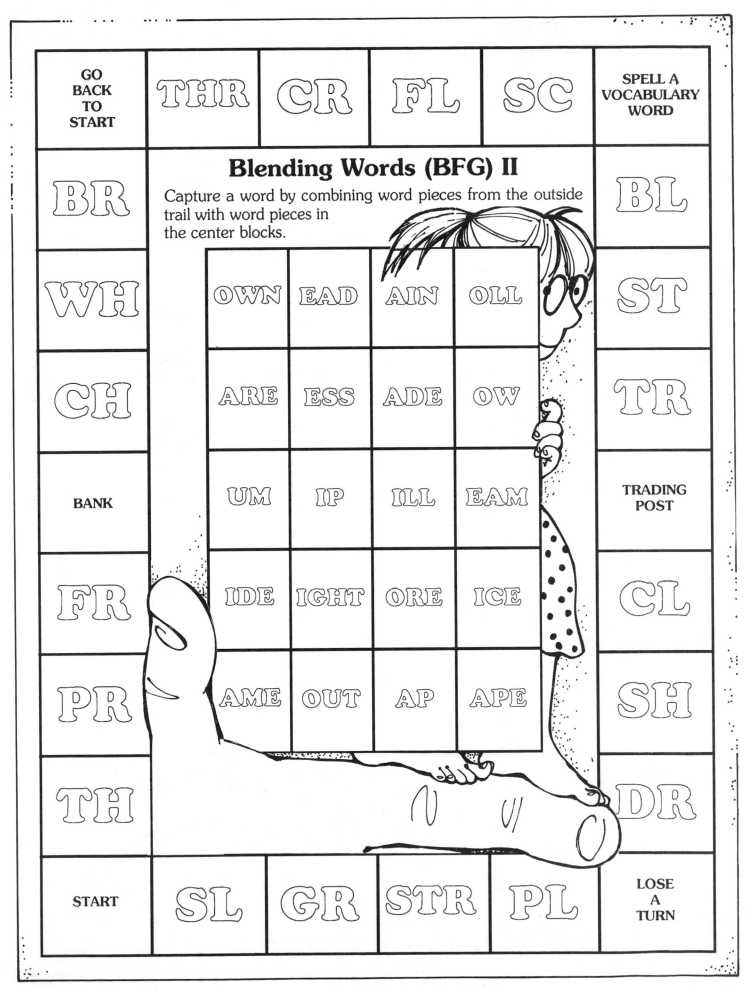

Blending Words (BFG) II

Capture a word by combining word pieces from the outside trail with word pieces in the center blocks.

OWN	EAD	AIN	OLL
ARE	ESS	ADE	OW
UM	IP	ILL	EAM
IDE	IGHT	ORE	ICE
AME	OUT	AP	APE

Outer trail:

GO BACK TO START — THR — CR — FL — SC — SPELL A VOCABULARY WORD

BR — BL

WH — ST

CH — TR

BANK — TRADING POST

FR — CL

PR — SH

TH — DR

START — SL — GR — STR — PL — LOSE A TURN

17

GA1459

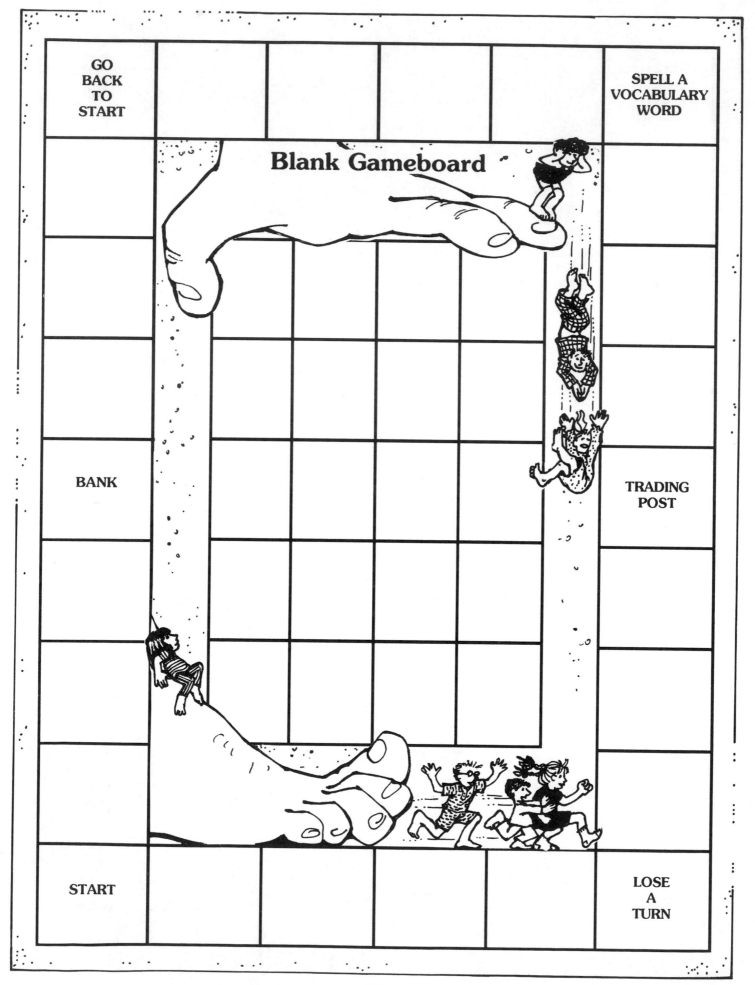

GO
BACK
TO
START

SPELL A
VOCABULARY
WORD

Blank Gameboard

BANK

TRADING
POST

START

LOSE
A
TURN

18

Fantastic Mr. Fox

Battle of Wits

Bean, Bunce, and Boggis

A Community

Food Search

Missing Tail

Animal Habitats Everywhere Tunnels

GA1459

Lead-Ins to Literature

You are a clever little fox. You are about to meet up with the three meanest farmers in your neighborhood. The farmers have vowed to get you, because you have been eating their chickens for years. When they come after you, you will be risking the lives of your children. The farmers may be wise to most of your tricks. Modern technology seems about ready to outsmart you. It is decision time. Leave the neighborhood and your home or . . . Oh, no! It's too late. Your house in the ground is surrounded by guns and steam shovels. There is no way out! Or is there?

1. What would attract readers to a story about a chicken-eating fox that is fighting the farmers that he steals from each night? _____

_____

_____

2. The farmers are painted as being mean and nasty. What three things do you think they did to get that kind of a reputation? _____

_____

_____

3. Where is the closest farmland to your school? Your home? Would farmers in your area have trouble with deer, foxes or burrowing animals? _____

_____

_____

4. Before starting the story, find three facts about the eating habits of a fox. See if your three research facts are mentioned in the story. _____

_____

_____

5. What are a fox's babies called? How are the babies raised? By both parents? One parent? What do they eat? _____

_____

_____

6. Burrowing animals can be found just about everywhere. What are their classifications and characteristics? What do the animals in the story have in common with the general population of burrowing animals found on a farm? _____

_____

_____

7. What animals would you expect to find in a Fox vs. Farmer paperback thriller book? _____

_____

_____

Predict the story's outcome in the space below, or illustrate on the back of this sheet.

_____

_____

_____

GA1459

Just the Facts

Can you write a question whose factual answer will be the word on the left of each line?

Example: Mr. Bunce/Whose ducks was Mr. Fox after?

1. The rat _____

2. The chicken house _____

3. Carrots _____

4. Drinking sunbeams and rainbows _____

5. The tunnel _____

6. The machines against the foxes _____

7. The miserable midget _____

8. Horrible crooks _____

Write a tercet highlighting a fact from the story. Here is an example:

> The fox had mud on his face.
> He was in a desperate race
> to save his underground place.

_____

_____

_____

Design a "Fantastic Mr. Fox" acrostic. Each letter should start a factual statement about the story.

F _____

A _____

N _____

T ractors attacked the hilltop in search of Mr. Fox. _____

A _____

S _____

T _____

I _____

C _____

M _____

R at wasn't too keen on sharing his hideout. _____

F _____

O _____

X cavations were made to find the fox family's den. _____

On the back of this sheet "acrostic-size" another character from the story. This time illustrate each letter.

21

What Is Your Opinion?

1. Most people would root for Mr. Fox in this story, probably because the author portrays the farmers as being mean and nasty. How do you think an average, friendly and likeable farmer feels about a fox eating the chickens each night? If a nice farmer was being attacked each night, would just as many people root for the farmer as for the fox? Why do you think so? _____
_____
_____

2. Did you think the tractors and mechanical shovels would get the fox when they were first introduced in the story? Why or why not? _____
_____
_____

3. How did you feel about the way the fox family was starving—or the "dig for your lives" shout to the family? _____
_____
_____

4. Mr. Fox's wife had a lot of confidence in her husband. What causes this to happen between two adults or friends? _____
_____
_____

5. Can you think of a more sensible strategy for the farmers than bulldozers to get rid of the fox family? (Please don't mention poison. Usually, it kills more animals than it is intended to kill. Besides, the fantastic Mr. Fox seems much too smart to be fooled by a poison.)_____
_____
_____

6. Bean the Rat's cider cellar adventure was a change of pace for the author. What was the neatest part of meeting this somewhat selfish rat halfway through the story? _____
_____
_____

7. Is there any type of fox that is on the endangered species list? How would this have changed the actions of the three farmers? _____
_____
_____

8. How would you rate the animal poetry (pages 14/83) that appears in the story? Critique one of the mini verses; then add some additional lines to two of them. _____
_____
_____

Write some opinion challenging questions on the back of this sheet.

GA1459

Drills for Skills

It shouldn't be that difficult to find the answers to these clues. Each answer has the letters *ox* in exact order in it. Place the correct answer in the answer blank.

Clue	**Answer**	**Illustration**

This *ox* is

1. a toy holder   box
2. an ox pair
3. a giant shrimp
4. a childhood disease
5. Frank Thomas's team
6. poisonous
7. an English college
8. earth's primary gas
9. steers a racing shell
10. sparring
11. found in the blood and fights disease
12. March 21 and September 23
13. small wagon
14. causes rust
15. high altitude must

Illustrate six of the answers in the boxes found on this page.

GA1459

Full of Word Sentences
Vexing Vocabulary

enormously	keen	clutch	smother
badger	especially	cautious	juicy
entrance	foggiest	mechanical	ravenous
furious	poison	dozed	surround
miraculous	plump	tunnel	caterpillar
moment	weasel	porch	barrel

How many of these vocabulary words can you squeeze into one sentence and still have the sentence make sense? List your ten best sentences in the blanks below. Then place the number of vocabulary words over the total words in the sentences to find your "fractional vocabulary."

1. The *badger* has an *especially keen* sense of smell.
   3 vocabulary words/over 9 total words or 1/3

2. _____
3. _____
4. _____
5. _____
6. _____
7. _____
8. _____
9. _____
10. _____

How many couplets can you write incorporating the vocabulary words in the rhyme or in the rhyme's body?

1. The picture on the easel/was one of a weasel.
2. It is hard to tunnel/with a hat-shaped funnel.
3. I love to smother/my darling mother/with kindness.
4. Why is Dad so furious?/I am, of course, overly curious.
5. The store was closed/so the employees just dozed.

Write your couplets or rhyme starters below.

GA1459

Short-Term Project I

The Paddington Bear Shop in London has every item that you can imagine. Paddington Bear of literature fame is featured in a thousand different situations on items ranging from sweaters to socks to mugs. You are the owner of such a shop. Pick an animal from the story and feature that animal on the six items given below. Three boxes remain for your own choices of objects to display your selected animal. On the back of the page make a large scale drawing of your best product.

25

GA1459

Business Shop License Application
Short-Term Project II

You are about to open a store similar to the Paddington Bear Shop in London. It can be called the Fantastic Mr. Fox Shop or feature any animal that you want to develop into a saleable item. Please fill out the questionnaire below before opening your business.

1. Your name _____

2. Your business name _____

3. The animal featured in your shop _____

4. Reason for your selection _____

5. Place a small sketch of your store logo in the box.

6. Location of your shop _____

   Street number/city/state _____

7. Bank financing was from what institution? _____

8. Describe the type of products you will be selling._____
   _____

9. Will live animals be sold on the premises? If so, please describe the procedures for their care and housing. _____
   _____
   _____

10. Store hours _____

11. Business assistants' names _____

12. Three local papers that will be running your ads _____
   _____
   _____

13. Your thirty-second radio spot will be as follows:_____
   _____
   _____
   _____

14. Most expensive store item _____

15. Least expensive store item _____

16. On the back of this page, describe your long-term goals for the business and for yourself. Do you plan to expand? Are you looking for early retirement? Are you leaving the business to family members or using it to pay for college?

GA1459

Ideas and Illustrations

Not too many states or countries use animals on their flags (California uses the bear). Six flags with animals from the story are shown below. Design each flag and then give information about the state/country it represents and why that flag is an appropriate choice. Copy your best drawings on large construction paper. Make an "animal flag" bulletin board with your classmates.

_____   _____

_____   _____

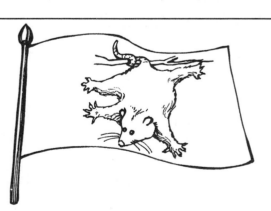

_____   _____

_____   _____

_____   _____

_____   _____

Use the back of this page to design a flag with the bald eagle as the centerpiece.

   GA1459

Student Research Suggestions

What type of information can you find to add to the body of knowledge surrounding the fox? Write a brief comment about each topic area below. Take the two most interesting areas and develop them into a two-part poster titled "The Fascinating Fox."

1. Kit foxes _____

_____

2. Arctic foxes _____

_____

3. Gray foxes _____

_____

4. Red foxes _____

_____

5. Fennecs _____

_____

6. South American "foxes" _____

_____

7. Bat-eared foxes _____

_____

8. Life expectancy _____

_____

9. Gestation period _____

_____

10. Care of young/Size of litter _____

_____

11. Fox dens _____

_____

12. Food preferences _____

_____

13. Hunting skills _____

_____

14. Children's stories featuring a fox _____

_____

GA1459

Teacher Suggestions

1. Review Aesop's fables with your class. After introducing and discussing the story "The Fox and the Grapes" have your class write a more modern parody using another article of their choice. Your class might want to write and illustrate modern fables on the following topics:

   The Fox and the Nike™ Sneakers
   The Fox and the Pizza Pie
   The Fox and the Four Speed Bike
   The Fox and Super Mario Brothers™
   The Fox and Michael Jackson
   Place each student story in a book for classroom display.

2. The changing American farm is an excellent idea for a classroom mural. Students should divide a piece of art paper into two sides. On the left they show the way things were done in the past. On the right they show the more modern approaches to farming. Create a flow chart which will show how food gets from a farm to a dinner table.

3. Create a "Dear Fantastic Fox" newspaper column. Each student creates an animal with a problem. Papers are exchanged and each student then writes the answer as Fantastic Mr. Fox.

4. Have your students design underground cities for people and animals. Discuss with your class the needs of each of these groups. Have each student include a short story on why people had to move underground to prosper or survive.

5. What Animals Can and Cannot Be Domesticated is a great discussion topic. Take an exotic pet survey. What strange creature would each student select for a pet and why?

6. Design menus that Mr. Fox would give to his animal friends, listing some of their favorite foods (Rat: Cheez Doodles™, Squirrel: hot fudge nut sundae, Badger: chicken gumbo, etc.)

7. Research sports teams that have animal mascots and symbols that might be found on the farm. Seventy percent of my boys did the Chicago Bulls. Wasn't the turkey suggested by Ben Franklin as our national symbol?

8. Research famous people that have *Fox* for their last name. My encyclopedia included Charles James Fox, George Fox and Paula Fox.

9. Make a "funny occupations" list with your students. Audrey Badger/Philadelphia complaint office, James Burgher/McDonald's, Natasha Brown/artist, Phil Bean/grocery store.

10. Story starter: "The Day I Was Outfoxed."

11. Keep a diary reflecting one day in the life of a fox.

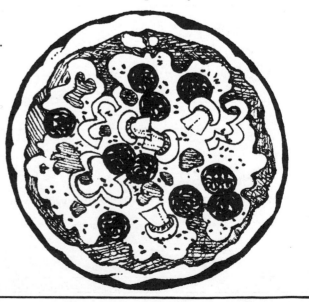

Write Like a Master

The theme for each story starter below is the American farmer, animal rights or cartoon animals. Try to vary your writing style in each story starter. Copy the starters on a page big enough to expand your stories and have enough room for a few illustrations.

Story Starter I

The American farmer is slowly being driven out of business by drought, poor crop prices, foreign produce and the inability to secure loans from the banking or private sector. Until all America wakes up and realizes that _____

_____

_____

_____

Story Starter II

Spinach is beginning to turn my whole body green. Everything my mother cooks and prepares has spinach in it. She saw this recipe book on a TV show, sent away for it, and now has changed my life forever. Last night it was applesauce tainted with spinach. Tonight she is planning something entirely different. It is spinach and _____

_____

_____

_____

Story Starter III

How can I be a cartoon character on this side of the room and a real person on the other side? This happened in the film *Cool World*. It can't possibly happen in the real world. If you stand in the exact middle of the room, half of your body looks real while the other half is cartoonish. I am trying to think of some type of benefit this condition will give me. Right now I can think of only two. _____

_____

_____

_____

Story Starter IV

Newspaper headline . . . Rabbit fever is sweeping Pottsville . . . the facts are gruesome. Adults and children have this awful_____

_____

_____

_____

Story Starter V

(Crazy Farmer) Ha! People will always win out over a scrawny little fox. Just wait until my secret weapon arrives. It _____

_____

_____

Public Speaking

You are responsible for a one-minute speech on any one of the topics below. There is a space after each topic for brief notes. This will give your teacher an opportunity to see that you are headed in the right direction before actually giving your speech.

1. You are explaining to a farmers' group the dangers of using poison to get rid of bothersome deer, gophers or foxes.

_____

_____

_____

2. You are giving a speech in a foxhole underground. You are explaining to your fellow animals the importance of sticking together for the good of the whole community.

_____

_____

_____

3. You are speaking on the worth of a particular vegetable. Your choices might include carrots, broccoli, spinach or any other of your favorites. Please include some actual research facts about your selected vegetable.

_____

_____

_____

4. You are a farmer standing over a foxhole. You are using your wits to talk a fox and his family out of their hole and out of the neighborhood.

_____

_____

_____

5. You are the guide at a natural science museum. You are standing in front of the museum's most important animal exhibit. Introduce the exhibit to your audience. Please make sure you have three props or pictures to correspond to your presentation.

_____

_____

_____

6. You are giving a speech to raise money for the protection of endangered species in your area. What species will you choose to introduce to your listening audience?

_____

_____

_____

Write three of your own speech topics related to animals on the back of this sheet.

GA1459

Gameboard

Materials Needed: Two number cubes, movers, light-colored crayons; Vexing Vocabulary; Just the Facts. Student-made and teacher-made question cards can be placed in areas around the gameboard. They are optional but highly recommended. A card is picked each time a player has a multiple of ten points in his or her bank. Players earn five points for each word recorded.

Players Needed: Two to four players or teams of two players

Play Procedures: Players alternate turns; throw number cubes; move in either direction at any time. This allows for playing strategies, rather than just mindlessly moving around a gameboard.

The Roll: Roll both number cubes. Your teacher will tell you to conduct some math operations with the number cubes. The three rules used most often in my classroom are

    a. Add the two cubes and move the number of spaces in the ones column. (6 + 6 = <u>12</u>. 2 in ones column; move two spaces.)

    b. Roll the two cubes and move ahead the larger number.

    c. Roll the two cubes and move ahead the smaller number.

Object: To score thirty-five points or to capture a box of four squares in the middle of the gameboard. This can be accomplished by landing on a word box in a normal turn, trading for word boxes when you land on a trading post or buying *one* of them for two times its value when you land on the bank. Each time you land on a word piece, you try to combine it with a piece in the middle to make a word. You can use the blank gameboard to create your own variations. Record your words in the bank below. Ownership will change after trades only. Cross them out on the score sheet and add them to the other column. A scoreboard is provided for you.

Winning: Words will vary. The game is designed so two or three words can be made from each landing area.

Player One's Words/Score	Player Two's Words/Score
Word Bank	**Word Bank**
1. _____	1. _____
2. _____	2. _____
3. _____	3. _____
4. _____	4. _____
5. _____	5. _____

GA1459

Plural Paths

ES	S	COMPLETELY DIFFERENT	ES
IES	IES	S	IES
S	STAYS THE SAME	ES	S
ES	IES	S	ES
ES	IES	S	IES

Outside trail (clockwise):

GO BACK TO START · SHOE · TRADING POST · STEM · BABY · SPELL A VOCABULARY WORD · TRACTOR · GOOSE · BOX · PICK A FACT CARD · PARTY · ROACH · PIE · LOSE A TURN · DEER · FAIRY · CHURCH · TOY · START · FACTORY · MONKEY · FLOWER · BANK · DITCH · FOX · STORY

Move on the outside trail. Cover up the plural ending for the word you land on. Four in a row wins. Person with the most squares covered wins, if four in a row isn't found.

33

GA1459

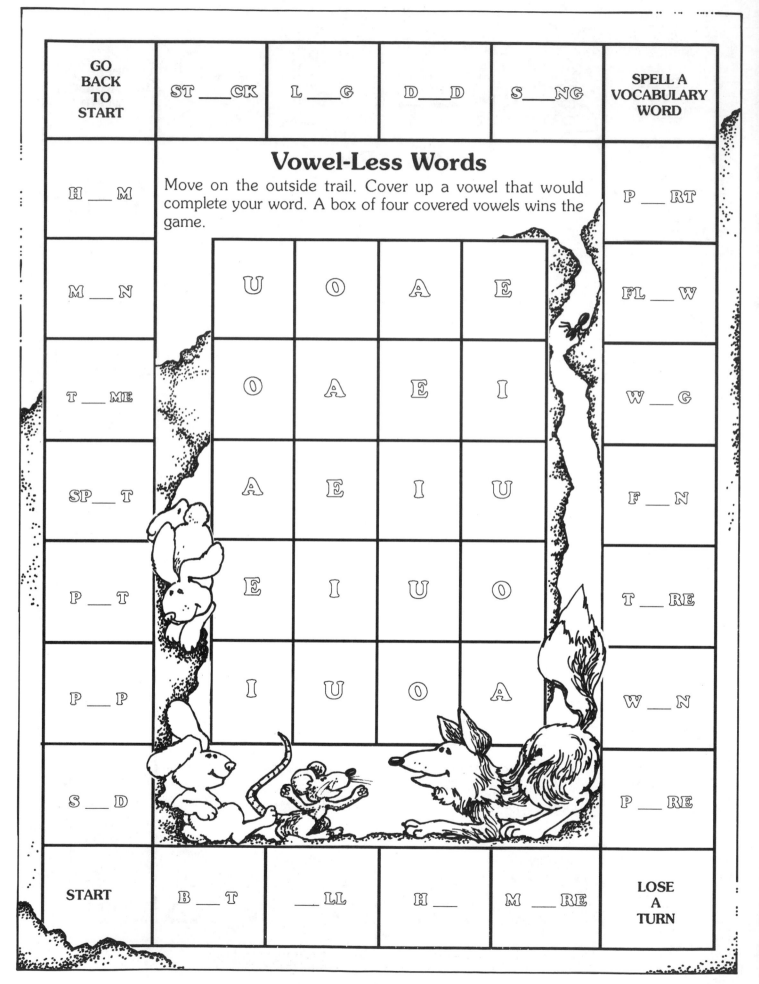

GO BACK TO START	ST ___ CK	L __ G	D__D	S___NG	SPELL A VOCABULARY WORD
H __ M					P __ RT
M __ N	U	O	A	E	FL __ W
T __ ME	O	A	E	I	W __ G
SP__ T	A	E	I	U	F __ N
P __ T	E	I	U	O	T __ RE
P __ P	I	U	O	A	W __ N
S __ D					P __ RE
START	B __ T	___ LL	H __	M __ RE	LOSE A TURN

Vowel-Less Words

Move on the outside trail. Cover up a vowel that would complete your word. A box of four covered vowels wins the game.

34

GA1459

James and the Giant Peach

Peach Surprise Aunt Sponge Tunnel Food

Insect Suggestions Rhinoceros Meal

Manhattan Surprise

GA1459

Lead-Ins to Literature

Most of us have heard the story of the giant beanstalk. You know . . . the one in Jack's yard. Few readers have heard the story of the giant peach that ate _____ (type in the name of your town or city). Your city had a far greater number of people in it until the killer peach came to town. This isn't make-believe. As soon as you read *James and the Giant Peach*, you'll find out things your family was afraid to tell you. If you frighten easily, make sure you turn the pages of the story very slowly.

1. What fruit would you create to grow to large proportions in your own backyard? _____
_____
_____

2. What humorous things could an author do with a peach that is rolling through the main street of your town? _____
_____
_____

3. Would you give this peach, or the fruit you have chosen, a voice in the story? Please explain why or why not. _____
_____
_____

4. Do you think this peach might be powered by some creature driving the peach from inside? What would you predict a good author might choose? _____
_____
_____

5. Can a peach be a friendly creature? Do you expect it to run around the countryside eating and crushing things? _____
_____
_____

6. How would you stop a runaway peach without bruising, damaging or destroying the peach?
_____
_____

7. Can you name three things that ordinarily are made with peaches? (Example: peach cobbler)
_____
_____

8. Can you make up three things that can be made with a giant peach? (Example, peach tree house, peach coach for Cinderella) _____
_____
_____

9. Where are most of the United States' peaches grown? _____
_____

10. What kind of climate is best for peach growing? _____
_____

Just the Facts

1. James had a good life with his parents. For how many years did this life last? _____

2. What three nasty things did Aunt Sponge and Aunt Spiker call James?

    a._____

    b._____

    c._____

3. The Giant Peach Monument was located in _____

4. Name at least four creatures that travelled with James and the peach. What part did they play in the story?

    a._____

    b._____

    c._____

    d._____

    e._____

5. Seagulls were going to help the giant peach out of danger. The _____ was going to be used as bait. This would allow the seagulls to be harnessed.

6. What was added to the jug from Jim's head?_____

7. The peach lost _____ when hit by the hailstones.

8. Write four facts about the inside of the giant peach.

    a._____

    b._____

    c._____

    d._____

9. Aunt Sponge declared that she looked and smelled like a _____. Aunt Spiker teased her about the way her _____ showed.

10. What was described as being about the size of a fox? _____

11. The centipede reported that a _____ was felt by everyone when the aunts were run over by the giant peach.

Write a fact about each of the following people and places:

The city of New York_____

The Old Green Grasshopper _____

The story's poems _____

The tiny green things_____

GA1459

What Is Your Opinion?

1. Do you think people will care more about insects after reading this story? Explain your ideas. _____

_____

2. Why do you think the peach is pictured as voiceless in this story? _____

_____

_____

3. A giant peach and a hungry rhino are things that I wouldn't want to be crushed under or eaten by. Name three other things that you wouldn't want to be crushed under or eaten by. Why?

   a. _____ _____

   b. _____ _____

   c. _____ _____

4. Can you think of three good reasons for living inside a peach?_____

_____

_____

5. James's early life seemed to be quite hard. His aunts treated him terribly, and knowing his parents were eaten by a giant rhino wasn't exactly calming. What type of personality do you think he had to enable him to get past all these problems? _____

_____

_____

6. How would you feel if your mean aunts were crushed by a giant peach? Would you feel differently if they were good people?_____

_____

_____

7. How did you feel about James's parents in this story? What good traits could they have taught their son in just four years? _____

_____

_____

8. What insect did you feel was portrayed as the most intelligent insect in the story? Why? ____

_____

_____

9. Animals are often used as rides in children's stories. How do you think young children will react to a character riding in a giant peach? _____

_____

_____

10. What would you have James and the giant peach do in a follow-up story? _____

_____

GA1459

Groups of consonants are listed below. The consonants are in the exact order in which they would appear in a word. You do not have to unscramble the letters like an anagram. Your job is to select a vowel that can be used to make each group of consonants into a word. To make the activity challenging, you can use only one vowel with each consonant cluster. That vowel can be placed anywhere among the consonants. You will need at least two or three of that same vowel (say three *a*'s) to make a word. Write what fraction of the whole word is made of vowels in the blank to the right of the new word.

Consonant Cluster	New Word	Fraction
Example: BNN	banana	$^3/_6$
1. KW		
2. PV		
3. SKNG		
4. BZR		
5. RVR		
6. SL		
7. CRVN		
8. VRGRN		
9. NT		
10. LSK		
11. NFNTY		
12. MRMR		
13. LV		
14. NDLY		
15. TMLT		

How many words can you find that use only one vowel in their construction? Make a list of the words that have two, three or four of this same vowel.

Two-Vowel Words	Three-Vowel Words	Four-Vowel Words

Vexing Vocabulary I

Here are some clues for words that have *each* or *ame* in them in exact order. See how many you can solve. Then use the space at the bottom of the page to create a new category or write five additional clues of your own for these same word parts.

This *ame*

1. is played on the playground _____
2. finds fault with _____
3. is slang for *woman* _____
4. is part of a large fire _____
5. is baseball players' hall _____
6. is two world land masses _____
7. is poor horse condition _____
8. is alike _____

This *each*

1. is a hole in the dam _____
2. is an arm's length measure _____
3. is a summer resting spot _____
4. is a clothes whitener _____
5. is to share words of wisdom _____
6. was Christa McAuliffe's profession _____
7. is a nectarine _____
8. is one another _____

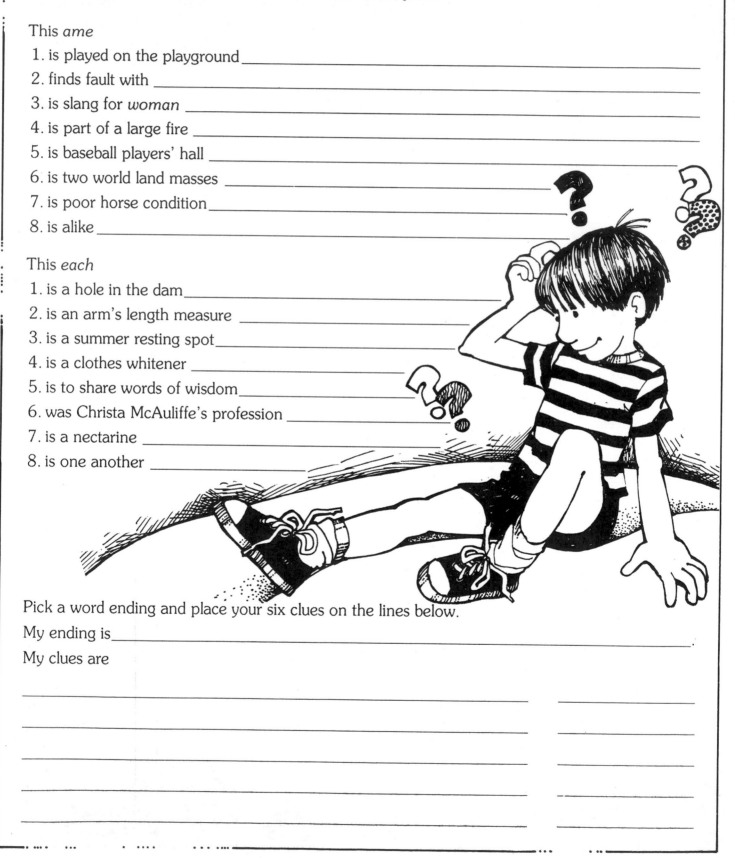

Pick a word ending and place your six clues on the lines below.

My ending is _____

My clues are

_____ _____

_____ _____

_____ _____

_____ _____

_____ _____

GA1459

Record Titles
Vexing Vocabulary II

centipede	elegant	nuisance	seagull
stomach	underneath	hallelujah	tiptoed
enormous	desolate	chaperone	London
hailstones	drowsily	faint	murmur
hobbled	tethered	swallow	bruised
delight	dazzling	massive	gorgon

You are an employee of a leading record company. One of your jobs is to create names for soon-to-be released albums. Each name must have at least one vocabulary word in it. If you use two words, that is even better. Place the names of the albums and the performers in the spaces provided below. Then draw illustrations for the new albums.

Album Name	Album Name	Album Name
Murmur from a Bruised Heart	*Elegant Delight*	
Recording Artist	**Recording Artist**	**Recording Artist**
Whitney Houston	Trisha Yearwood	

Album Name	Album Name	Album Name
Recording Artist	**Recording Artist**	**Recording Artist**

41

GA1459

Short-Term Project

Fruits, vegetables and other foods are often used to describe people, situations and assorted events. Design a food phrase file below. See how many expressions you can identify for each item. Illustrate your three favorites on the flip side of the page.

Pea
1. They are like two peas in a pod.
2. He has a brain the size of a pea.

Peach
1. Well, isn't that peachy!
2. She is a real peach.

Cherry
1. _____
2. _____

Whipped Cream
1. The team was creamed 45-0.
2. That pony is the cream of the crop of last year's foals.

Plum
1. _____
2. _____

Apple
1. Johnny was the apple of her eye.
2. That is the largest Adam's apple I have ever seen.

Strawberry
1. _____
2. _____

Lemon
1. That used car was a lemon.
2. Their relationship soured for no apparent reason.

Banana
1. _____
2. _____

Cheese
1. He thinks he is a big cheese on the baseball diamond.
2. Gouda night, my darling.

Your choice of food item _____
1. _____
2. _____

Your choice of food item _____
1. _____
2. _____

GA1459

Ideas and Illustrations

You are the designer of containers for a host of new products that have peaches in them. Colorfully design the containers in the spaces provided below. Then place your best products on larger pieces of paper. Hang these peach products on a classroom clothesline. The items you will design containers for are:

1. a cover for a book with peaches as the theme
2. a jar for peach face cream
3. a bottle for peach shampoo
4. a record album cover for the new group The Peaches
5. a box for a peach toy
6. a wrapper for peach candy

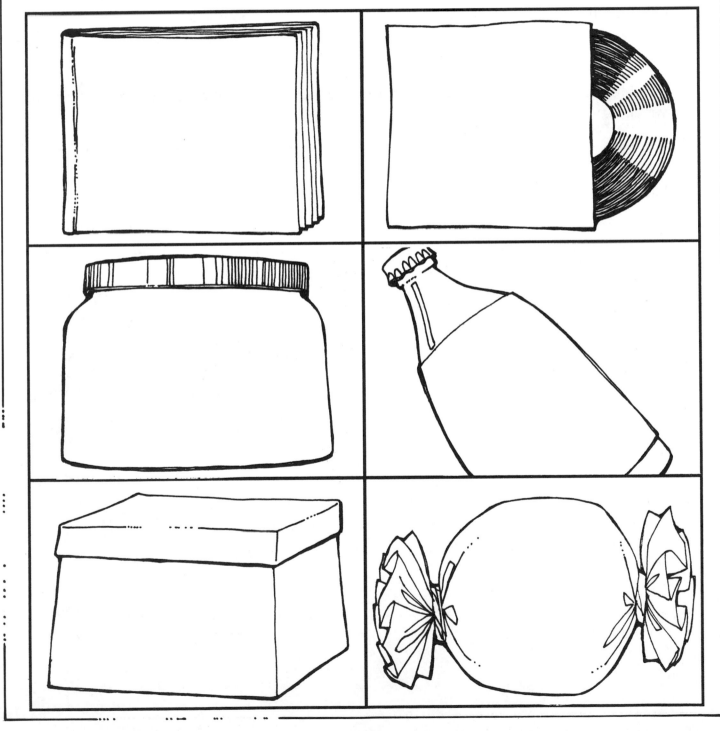

GA1459

Student Research Suggestions

Select a fruit or vegetable to research and share with the class. The presentation of your research may include dressing up as the fruit or vegetable of your choice. You don't have to be that fruit or vegetable, but you do have to incorporate it in your costume. Answering the following questions about peaches will help get you started on your fruit and vegetable exploration.

1. The peach was first grown in China thousands of years ago. How, then, did it get the name the "Persian apple"? _____

    _____

    _____

2. What are the differences between a peach, a nectarine, and an apricot?_____

    _____

    _____

3. Peaches are classified as *freestone* or *clingstone*. What is the difference between these two varieties of peaches? _____

    _____

    _____

4. How does our country compare to the rest of the world in peach production?_____

    _____

    _____

5. What can you share with your classmates about the peach growing industry in California? __

    _____

    _____

6. Peaches bloom very early. Why is this dangerous? _____

    _____

    _____

7. Are more peaches canned or eaten fresh throughout the world? ___

    _____

    _____

8. List additional facts from your research on peaches._____

    _____

    _____

    _____

    _____

9. On the back list three topics that could be researched while reading *James and the Giant Peach*.

Teacher Suggestions

1. Give each child a giant, round piece of orange paper on which to design the interior of James's peach. Other fruit or vegetable interiors may also be chosen: red for a giant apple, yellow for a giant lemon, green for a giant pea. Have the children make up mini episodes telling what would happen inside their new vehicles.

2. Invite someone from the local food administration office to talk about food inspection and proper handling during shipping. Maybe you'll be lucky and find a food inspector in your school.

3. Discuss with your class the odes and dedications that were written by early poets (Ode to a Grecian Urn; Tiger, Tiger, Burning Bright). Give them copies of easy-to-understand odes or dedications and ask your students to mimic the writing style and phrasing with a fruit as the theme.

   Apple, apple, so shiny and bright.
   Oh! What a taste late at night.

   O' sour lemon
   A taste bitter but true.
   My lips tell me
   Not to forget you.

   To the grape–
   You've made happy lips, purple tongues and filled stomachs.

   Spinach and other greens
   How you've tormented me
   But healthy I'll grow up to be.

4. After teaching the characteristics of a fruit and vegetable, take a class poll or survey to find out:
   a. the best/least liked fruit or vegetable
   b. most/least eaten
   c. most/least expensive by the pound
   d. traveled the farthest/least to your table
   e. strangest fruit or vegetable in appearance and size

5. Have your class make an illustrated dictionary of fruit jokes. Each page features a fruit and an illustrated joke. (Example: What is purple and goes bam, bam, bam, bam? A four-door grape. How can seventeen people divide four apples? Make applesauce. Knock, knock. Who's there? Orange. Orange who? "Orange" you coming out to play?)

6. Discuss the true story of Johnny Appleseed. Have your class make comparisons to *James and the Giant Peach*.

7. Research the process for making dried fruit. Discuss the benefits and disadvantages of using dried fruit. Design a class bulletin board titled "From Grape to Raisin."

8. Develop a Roald Dahl questionnaire with your class that can be given to students throughout the school. Focus on questions that might lead new students to read Roald Dahl. (Example: Do you know the Roald Dahl book that proves witches really live today? Are you familiar with the five bone-crushing stories? Do you know the size of the largest peach ever grown? Do you believe that one day animals will communicate with humans?)

9. Your science program can be enhanced with lessons on fruit spoilage. Is it true that the more sugar in a fruit, the faster it spoils? (Recording observations and graphs on spoilage time came out professional looking with our "Mecc Graph" computer program. The downside was the gnats attacking our bananas each day.)

10. Design the wrappers for three fruity candy bars.

11. Design a race car that has fruit for its logo. Create oil, gas and tire companies for the race car.

Write Like a Master

Each writing topic follows the themes contained in *James and the Giant Peach*. Imagine you are the author of a similar book. Re-create the characters and the events in the story starters the way Roald Dahl would have written them.

Story Starter I

The giant boulder is ten feet from the baby carriage. I have to think of something to stop it. What if _____

_____

_____

_____

Story Starter II

This peach jam is outrageous. If you smear it on a rash, the rash disappears. If you put it in the hub of your bike's wheel, the bike moves faster and more smoothly. The jam even took an ink stain out of Dad's jacket. The jam came_____

_____

_____

_____

Story Starter III

Why, you ask, is this giant peach chasing me? Well, here is my story. It is not, as you can see, as unbelievable as it sounds. A great many of my classmates are witnesses. The _____

_____

_____

_____

Story Starter IV

Everything thrown in that fruit dish immediately becomes and stays invisible. Last week I tried fruit and candy. My teacher didn't see me eating chocolate bars all day. This week I threw a dictionary in there. It really helped me on my spelling test. Maybe the fruit dish could be put to more honest use. What do you think throwing a _____

_____

_____

Story Starter V

Rolling around inside this peach is making me dizzy. Maybe _____

_____

_____

_____

Public Speaking

Use the spaces below for speech planning. Your brief notes will allow your teacher to check the progress of your speech. At the bottom of the page list your own peach topics. You are responsible for giving a one or two-minute speech on the following topics:

1. You own a fruit stand and are giving a mini speech to a customer on the importance of peaches in a good diet.

_____

_____

2. A giant peach is crushing everything in sight. You are a scientist who wants the peach saved. You feel that the secret to its giant size will help alleviate the world's food shortages. You have to convince the local authorities to capture the peach and not destroy this possible food source.

_____

3. Your peach jam won first prize at the county fair. Compose your acceptance speech.

_____

_____

4. You are playing baseball in the house. An errant throw breaks Mom's favorite dishware. What will you say to her?

_____

_____

5. You are a baby who hates strained peaches. Mom has never heard you talk before, but you are going to give Mom a glowing piece of your mind about too many peaches.

_____

_____

6. You are allergic to peaches and have to explain to your doctor the strange growth that is all over your body.

_____

_____

7. You are presenting a new knife to a group of housewives, butchers and houseware department heads. The knife will cut through just about anything. It has a new cut protector which is part of the knife's newest features.

_____

_____

8. You are thanking people at your retirement dinner.

_____

_____

List your speech topics below.

GA1459

Building Words with Walking Vowels
Gameboard

Materials Needed: Separate colored disks for each team. If the gameboard is to be used only once, colored crayons could be used for children to claim and color in their personal or team's selection. Number cubes are needed to calculate the roll. Each time the cubes are rolled some operation with the two numbers should be performed. Student movers for each team to progress around the gameboard are also needed.

Players Needed: Two teams consisting of one or two players each. If the game is greatly enlarged, more players could be involved.

Play Procedure: Movers are placed at Start and can be moved in either direction at anytime in the game. This always gives the player two choices each time he or she moves.

Object: To land on a word with blanks on the outside trail and combine that box's offering with two vowels that will form a word from the inside region. Each time you use something from the inner region, that box becomes yours. You can color it with your team's colors or place a color marker on it to represent your team. As the game progresses, it becomes harder and harder to find matching word pieces.

Winning: Each time the game is played, the rule for a win can be changed. The rules most often used as a sign of victory are
    a. four boxes in a row (same team)
    b. a box of four (same team)
    c. a box of four (two from each team)
    d. Each word made counts five points. Whoever has the most points at the end of the game wins.

Additional Variations: Grab all words. When you land on an outside piece, every inner piece that can be used to make a word becomes your property. Victory is determined by who has the most words or who selects the last piece left in the board's interior. Anything studied in your classroom can be put on this type of gameboard.

GA1459

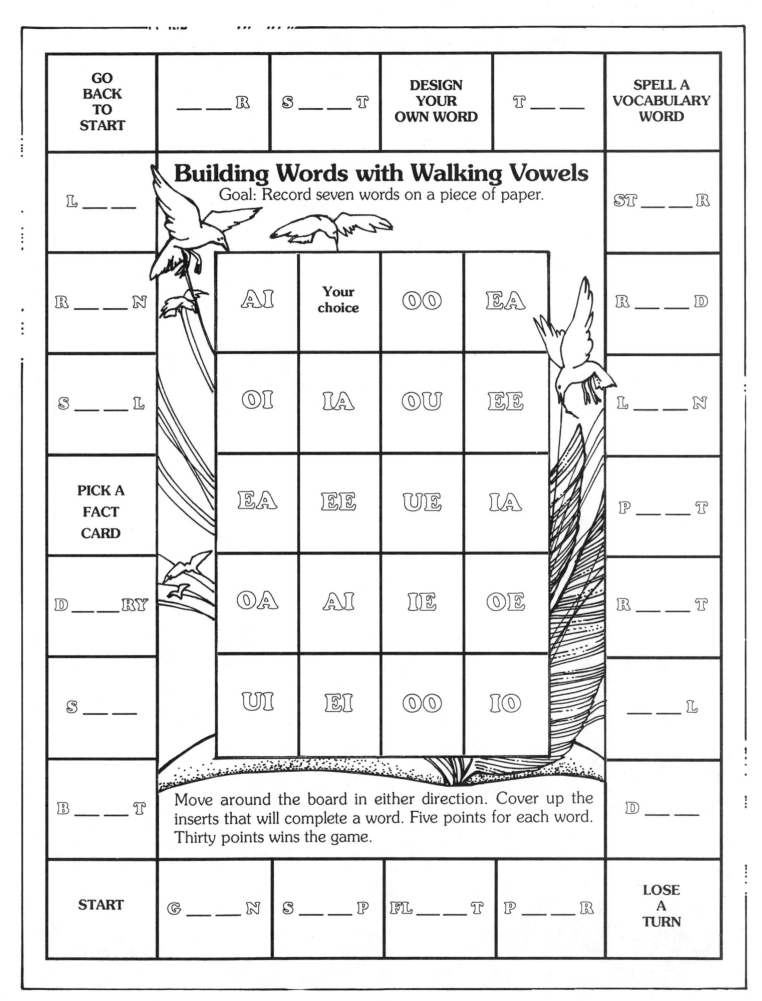

Building Words with Walking Vowels
Goal: Record seven words on a piece of paper.

GO BACK TO START	_ _ R _	S _ _ _ T	DESIGN YOUR OWN WORD	T _ _ _	SPELL A VOCABULARY WORD
L _ _ _					ST _ _ _ R
R _ _ _ N	AI	Your choice	OO	EA	R _ _ _ D
S _ _ _ L	OI	IA	OU	EE	L _ _ _ N
PICK A FACT CARD	EA	EE	UE	IA	P _ _ _ T
D _ _ _ RY	OA	AI	IE	OE	R _ _ _ T
S _ _ _	UI	EI	OO	IO	_ _ _ L
B _ _ _ T					D _ _ _

Move around the board in either direction. Cover up the inserts that will complete a word. Five points for each word. Thirty points wins the game.

START	G _ _ _ N	S _ _ _ P	FL _ _ _ T	P _ _ _ R	LOSE A TURN

49

GA1459

The Witches

Grandmother's

Wisdom Norwegian Tales Leif, the Porpoise

Spells Bruno, the Mouse Grand High Witch

Formula 86 Remove Your Gloves'

50

GA1459

Lead-Ins to Literature

One second Grandmother and her seven-year-old grandson are talking about "real life" witch tales. The next second the grandson is a mouse and Grandmother is entering the Grand High Witch's room trying to find the secret that will bring her grandson back to human form. I know you don't believe in witches. I didn't either. That is, until I followed Grandmother on her quest to rid the world of the Grand High Witch's evil. This would seem easy for us to do, but some strange happenings almost destroy them and all the world's children. If you feel that young people and grandmothers, without any help, should chase after witches, then read on. I don't want to ruin the story for you, but it is impossible to get rid of a witch.

1. What are the first three things that come to mind when someone mentions that witches are involved in a story?
   a. _____
   b. _____
   c. _____

2. If you designed a witch for a story, what three special powers would you give her? How would her powers differ if she were young or old? Would it matter where she lived?
   a. _____
   b. _____
   c. _____

3. What witch tales have you read before this particular story? Were these stories read to you, or did you read them on your own? Which was the scariest of those mentioned? _____
   _____
   _____

4. The Hotel Magnificent is a strange name for a hotel. List five places in your area that would make good meeting places for witches who are looking for someplace to hold their annual meeting. _____
   _____
   _____

5. What are three things that you might advise Grandmother to do before starting out to capture the Grand High Witch? _____
   _____
   _____

6. Would you accept a stranger's offer for chocolates, even if it was in a room that seated hundreds of people? See if you can make a humorous and serious reason for accepting or not accepting the Grand High Witch's offer. _____
   _____
   _____

7. What are the first three things you would have said when you found yourself face to face with a witch? What would your mother have said when you told her of the meeting? _____
   _____
   _____

8. Design a witch acrostic before starting the story. Make a prediction of story events.
   W _____
   I _____
   T _____
   C _____
   H _____

Just the Facts

1. One child a week is fifty-two children a year.
   Squish them and squiggle them and make them disappear.

   What is this couplet? _____

2. What nationality was Grandmother? _____

3. What did Grandmother say was the best part of a shrimp? _____

4. Bruno was bribed with _____ by the Grand High Witch.

5. Whose voice did Grandmother imitate? _____

6. "There she is! There she is feeding the ducks." Who was the statement about and what
   unbelievable happening caused these shrieks to occur? _____

7. What does the acronym RSFTPOCTC stand for? _____

   _____

8. What was Mr. Stringer's occupation? _____

9. How many real witches are probably still living in London today? _____

10. One of the important reasons for finding the castle was that it contained the _____
    of all the witches in the world. The Grand High Witch had to have all these addresses
    because it was the only way she could _____ the witches for the annual meeting.

11. Which country had the most witches, Norway or England? _____

12. A bottle of Formula 86 Delayed Mouse Maker contains _____ doses.
    If two hundred and fifty thousand children lived in England, how many bottles would be
    needed to turn all the children into mice? _____

13. Before meeting with Mr. and Mrs. Jenkins, Bruno was placed in a _____,
    where he managed to get fatter and fatter, thanks to _____ bananas.

14. The Hotel _____ was located in the famous seashore town of

    _____.

15. Grandmother gave her grandson two pet mice. What were their names? _____

16. The Grand High Witch did not want to accept "we'll do better" from the witches in the ball-
    room. She wanted only _____ results from them.

Below write the three facts that you think are most important to understanding the story.

_____

_____

_____

52

GA1459

What Is Your Opinion?

1. How did you feel when Grandmother offered her seven-year-old grandson a cigar? Did you laugh when she said it was good to smoke cigars as protection from colds? Explain. _____
_____

2. Was the picture Roald Dahl painted of the Grand High Witch a scary one? Explain. _____
_____

3. What do you think the author meant when he said that witches have magic in their fingers and devilry dancing in their blood?_____
_____

4. Which of the five witch happenings that Grandmother told about did you find most creative and enjoyable? _____
_____

5. Can you give three good reasons why large numbers of witches have never been caught at their annual meetings?_____
_____

6. You are on a witch hunt. Using the knowledge you gained from this book, what items would you take with you? What type of protection from magic spells do you recommend be taken on such a journey? _____
_____

7. Catching fifty-two children a year takes a great deal of cunning and planning. What "you are now captured" witch tricks do you feel will fool most of your friends? Why?_____
_____

8. If a witch is zapped at every annual meeting, how would the witches feel about going? Why?
_____
_____

9. Why do you think there aren't any male witches in this book? Would evil deeds be more frightening if performed by a male witch? Explain who is scarier. _____
_____

10. In many of his stories, Roald Dahl seems to always be doing something nasty to mean-spirited people, especially boys (Bruno, Charlie's companions in the chocolate factory). How could this be related to the author's own life? Give some possible reasons why this theme keeps appearing in Dahl's books. _____
_____

11. The Hotel Magnificent is a catchy name for a resort. What other things in your area have names that are appealing to you? _____
_____

53

GA1459

Vexing Vocabulary

curvy	wig	triumph	briefcase
bald	pistol	thumb	conscious
madam	delayed	corridor	flipper
actual	altered	murderer	kettle
eighty	entire	brilliant	grasp
fjord	reeled	panic	taxi

Use the vocabulary words above and enter them into the four categories listed below. If you use one word in a comment, score five points; two vocabulary words, score ten points; three words, score twenty points.

Witch Commandments

1. Thou shalt not *murder* children. You may crush, squiggle or *alter* them. 10 points
2. _____ _____ points
3. _____ _____ points
4. Thou shalt not *panic* in difficult situations. You will *triumph* over all children. _____ points
5. _____ _____ points

Witch Hints of Good Conduct

1. Never put your *thumb* out to catch a *taxi*. 10 points
2. Always *grasp* unruly children by the hair. 5 points
3. _____ _____ points
4. _____ _____ points
5. _____ _____ points

Witch Mottos

1. *Bald* is beautiful. 5 points
2. A *brilliant* witch is a joy forever. 5 points
3. _____ _____ points
4. _____ _____ points
5. Two *wigs* are better than one. _____ points

Favorite Witch Song Titles

1. "*Delayed* Mouse Boogie"; "*Briefcase* Surprises" 10 points
2. _____ _____ points
3. _____ _____ points
4. _____ _____ points
5. _____ _____ points

Write your own category and vocabulary word usage comments on the back of this sheet.

First-Letter Songs and Rhymes
Drills for Skills

The letters below start the first few words in songs and nursery rhymes that everyone should know. Write the complete words under each. Place the next line under it in both initial letters and words. Then make up five of your own to share with a classmate. You may want to focus on popular songs after you have exhausted all the nursery rhymes. Write the first eight letters of a song and place the artist's name in parentheses to narrow the solver's choices. Illustrate your three favorite selections on the back of this page.

Example: OSCYSBTDEL

Oh! Say, can you see, by the dawn's early light

WSPWHATTLG

What so proudly we hailed at the twilight's last gleaming

1. BBBSHYAW (Baa, baa, black sheep have you any wool)

_____

_____

2. GBALTIL

_____

_____

3. TWAOWWLIAS

_____

_____

4. HDDTCATF

_____

_____

5. OKCWAMOS

_____

_____

6. PPHPPCPPITP

_____

_____

7. LMMSOATEHCAW

_____

Try these on the back of this paper.
JAJWUTH
MHALLIFWWAS
RABBITT
JSCENFHWCENL
GPPAPKTGAMTC
HDDTMRUTC
HDSOAWHDHAGF

Teacher Note: Consider putting these on the chalkboard two at a time for the class to copy. Each time one is solved a new one is put up to replace it. The solver gives only one word at a time and, hopefully, a new person will discover the secret and give the next word.

Ideas and Illustrations

You are the owner of a Halloween costume shop. Business hasn't been that great because everything seems to be the same as you have been selling for years. You are about to go on a super campaign to advertise some new outfits. Design each Halloween costume below, and give a brief statement describing the key features.

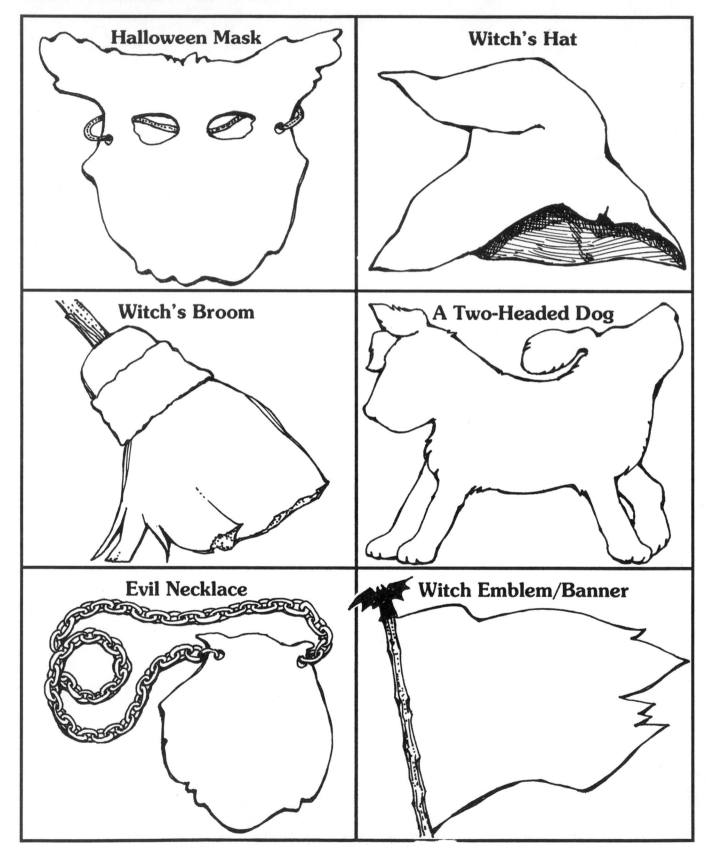

Halloween Mask

Witch's Hat

Witch's Broom

A Two-Headed Dog

Evil Necklace

Witch Emblem/Banner

GA1459

The Broom Pointer Puzzle
Short-Term Project

The head witch put her private letters in code to each of her witch companions around the world. The reasons for this secrecy are, of course, obvious. Each witch has the alphabet grid below. Start at the given letter and follow the way the brooms are pointed. See if you can decode the witch messages below. Then write the next messages in code before you make up some of your own.

Teacher Note: Place this grid on the chalkboard and give secret messages before starting the work sheet.

O	F	W	G	M
X	N	A	R	H
E	P	V	K	QZ
Y	B	J	T	D
L	I	S	C	U

Example: F➡ , S⬅ , U↘ , T⬇ , R➡ = witch

Decode these messages.

1. I➡ , K⬇ , F⬅ , Y↗ =

2. R➡ , D⬇ , A➡ , H⬅ , P↗ =

3. G⬇➡ , O⬇⬇ , V↗↗ , S↖⬆ =

4. V↗↘ , V↖↖ , V↗↗ , V⬇➡➡ =

5. C⬆ , Z⬆ , B⬇ , X➡ , G⬇⬇ =

Put these messages in code.

1. Save me. _____

2. Get back. _____

3. Look out. _____

4. Beware. _____

5. The end. _____

Write three sentences in code. Exchange them with classmates.

GA1459

i. Wishing on a wishbone stems from the belief that a chicken's body houses good spirits. When you consume a chicken, the good luck goes into the bones. Breaking the wishbone with a friend allows this good luck to be granted to the person holding the larger piece of the bone. There is, of course, more power in this piece. This extra power will insure the wish.

j. Giving hearts on Valentine's Day shares the belief that a heart is the center of truth. By giving you this truth, you will know that I really love you. (holidays, biology)

k. Rabbits' feet were carried by early people because of the respect they had for the rabbit's swiftness. They thought that the rabbit's hind legs contained this power.

l. Friday the thirteenth may have come from Norwegian folklore. The Norwegians believed that twelve key witches and the devil met on a Friday. (We added this to Grandmother's stories of Norwegian witches in the book *The Witches*. Numerology)

m. There is a belief that wearing garlic around your neck prevents you from having colds. What it might really do is keep people away from you so there is little chance of catching a cold.

n. The word *lunatic* may have come from an old superstition. If you stare at the moon too long, you will become crazy. *Luna* means "moon" in Latin, hence *lunatic*.

2. Illustrate a good wish clothesline with your class.

3. Research the origins of magic amulets and good luck charms. Invite students to design their own.

4. Divide a sheet of art paper in half. The left side should contain the perfect hotel room for young children. By contrast, the right side should contain what *every* witch would demand for her room.

5. Your class has found the address of the Grand High Witch. Ask students to write letters to her.

Write Like a Master

The theme for the story starters below revolves around a witch visiting your house, school or job. The witch could be dressed as a witch or in disguise. She could even be a talking cat, dog, mouse or animal of your choice.

Story Starter I
No witch story is an easy one. I learned how to recognize witches with the help of an old book that my grandfather left me. He claimed that the smartest witches from around the world met in Moorestown every five years. Their coven or witch group would try to get young children to____

_____

_____

_____

Story Starter II
Watch it grow! Her teeth are coming through the sides of her mouth. It is the worst thing that I have ever seen. I found this cave hidden under the maple tree. The maple tree is next to the pond, and the pond is always bubbling. The gases from the pond have done some strange things to the animals and babies in this area. Mr. Brier's daughter was _____

_____

_____

_____

Story Starter III
Mom and Dad won't let me dress up as a witch for Halloween. They keep talking about little Amy Pierce who dressed up as a witch five years ago and _____

_____

_____

_____

Story Starter IV
Explain what "witch work" is. Our office has never had a witch working in it before. What makes you think you are a witch? You seem like the rest of us except for _____

_____

_____

_____

Story Starter V
The witch cast an "opposite spell" on me. Some of the things that you have already noticed are that my sentences are written backward, my right arm moves forward when my

_____

_____

Public Speaking

Test your brainpower as you try to put together notes for a two-minute speech on one of the following topics:

1. You are the head witch at the annual witches' convention taking place in your town. What will you say to this gathering in your opening speech?

2. You are a salesperson who is selling a potion that is guaranteed to keep witches away from your family and home.

3. You sell hats and clothing to a very select group of people–witches. Give your classmates your best sales pitch for new items coming out this fall in your store.

4. You are talking about the importance of grandmothers.

5. You are the real estate salesperson that has to sell the Grand High Witch's castle.

6. You are the creator of a new game that features witches as the game's central theme.

7. You are giving a speech to Congress, trying to get Halloween declared a national holiday.

8. You are the favorite storyteller of a group of young children. You have finished one book but want to give them a brief taste of what you will be reading to them next week.

9. Enigmatology, the study of puzzles, is your favorite area. You just solved the secret of the Sphinx, Loch Ness Monster, Yeti, Bigfoot or some other mystery.

10. Norway's National Travel Foundation has hired you to promote tourism in their country. What type of presentation would you give a teachers' group about Norway? The group is looking for a summer travel location.

11. Convince your classmates that you have had an encounter with a real-life witch.

12. Witch Breath is a new mouth freshener. Describe this product's special traits to a group of potential users.

To make your speech more interesting, hang up three drawings behind you. You can make reference to the pictures while you are speaking. You may want to bring in props or something three-dimensional that can be referred to or used in your speech too.

Witch Numerology
Gameboard

Materials Needed: Separate colored disks for each team. If the gameboard is to be used only once, colored crayons could be used for children to claim and color in their personal or team's selection. Number cubes are needed to calculate the roll. Each time the cubes are rolled, some operation with the two numbers should be performed. Student movers for each team to progress around the gameboard are also needed.

Players Needed: Two teams consisting of one or two players each. If the game is greatly enlarged, more players could be involved.

Play Procedure: Movers are placed at Start and can be moved in either direction at anytime in the game. This always gives the player two choices each time he or she moves.

Object: To land on a number in the squares on the outside trail and combine that box's offering with the math category that will satisfy the number from the inside region. Each time you use something from the inner region, that box becomes yours. You can color it with your team's colors or place a color marker on it to represent your team. As the game progresses, it becomes harder and harder to find matching mathematical answers.

Winning: Each time the game is played, the rule for a win can be changed. The rules most often used as a sign of victory are
  a. four boxes in a row (same team)
  b. a box of four (same team)
  c. a box of four (two from each team)
  d. Total the value of the numbers that you correctly matched in the outside region. Whoever has the most points when no move remains wins.

Additional Variations: Grab all numbers. When you land on an outside piece, every inner piece that can be used to match that number becomes your property. Victory is determined by who has the most pieces or who selects the last piece left in the board's interior. Any math operation studied in your classroom can be put on this type of gameboard. Use the Blank Master for this purpose. Reduce fractions or practice drill facts.

GA1459

GO BACK TO START	125	72	18	228	SPELL A VOCABULARY WORD

Witch Numerology

Move on the outside trail. Cover up a matching answer on the inner region. The highest total of outside numbers wins.

324				67

9	A Prime	Divisible by 4	A Square Number	A Prime	144

169	A Cube	An Odd Number	A Factor of 36	Divisible by 6	10

220	Divisible by 10	A Factor of 35	Divisible by 3	An Even Number	6

5	Divisible by 11	A Square Number	A Factor of 24	A Cube	235

96	An Odd Number	Divisible by 5	An Even Number	A Twin Prime	81

12				64

START	44	13	7	31	LOSE A TURN

GA1459

The Twits

65

Just the Facts

Please write two facts that will become good questions for each of the topics below.

The appearance of Mr. Twit's beard

Fact 1: _____

Fact 2: _____

Foolery with a glass eye

Fact 1: _____

Fact 2: _____

The tree adventures of four sticky little boys

Fact 1: _____

Fact 2: _____

Muggle Wump and his "delightful" family

Fact 1: _____

Fact 2: _____

The use of glue for capturing purposes

Fact 1: _____

Fact 2: _____

Everything you could ask about body hair in the story

Fact 1: _____

Fact 2: _____

Mr. Twit's most creative ideas

Fact 1: _____

Fact 2: _____

What are the five most interesting facts that you can find out about Roald Dahl? Record them below.

1. _____

2. _____

3. _____

4. _____

5. _____

What Is Your Opinion?

1. Is it hard to like someone that is disgusting? Why or why not? Where do you think Mrs. Twit met Mr. Twit? Do you think he was that way when she met him? Explain. _____

_____

_____

2. What, in your opinion, are the three most disgusting traits of Mr. and Mrs. Twit? Did you laugh at their disgusting traits, or did you think that they weren't funny?

   a. _____

   b. _____

   c. _____

3. Can you give three easy-to-follow solutions to Mr. Twit's beard problem? How would you feel as the barber that had to trim his food-filled beard? _____

_____

_____

4. Do you think that guns are a good solution to the bird problem? Why or why not?_____

_____

_____

5. What do you think the Twits' children would be like? Do you think they would be just like their parents, or do you think the author would make them spotless to contrast the way their parents were? Explain. _____

_____

_____

6. If someone told you the Twits were coming to visit for the weekend, how would you prepare for them? _____

_____

_____

7. Why do some authors use unusual names for their characters, like Muggle Wump and Roly-Poly? _____

_____

_____

8. If you were writing the ending to *The Twits*, would you have had them disappear? Why or why not? _____

_____

9. What is the worst trait of all the characters in the story?

_____

10. What additional characters would you add to make the story more interesting? _____

_____

_____

GA1459

Vexing Vocabulary

sprinkled	cement	sleeve	hoist
train	language	parachute	sardine
lightest	revive	cabinet	extra
nail	morsel	fiery	stew
horrid	bare	demon	claw
perch	scissors	glimpse	cylinder

Because of their multiple meanings, many words taken out of context give few clues to their meaning in the original story. Write two sentences for each word below showing two different meanings for each word. Place a star next to the meaning that is closest to the way it was intended to be used in *The Twits*.

Example:

perch
1. The perch is a freshwater fish.
2. The bird was knocked off its perch by the strong wind.

parachute
1. _____
2. _____

claw
1. _____
2. _____

sardine
1. _____
2. _____

train
1. _____
2. _____

stew
1. _____
2. _____

hoist
1. _____
2. _____

cement
1. _____
2. _____

extra
1. _____
2. _____

Drills for Skills

The story *The Twits* is an excellent jumping off point for activities that reinforce words that have *tw* in them. Although most of the clues below have answers that start with *tw*, some have the *tw* in different positions. After you read the clue and find the correct answer, see if you can write a second clue that will generate the same word. Your hint may be better than the one originally given.

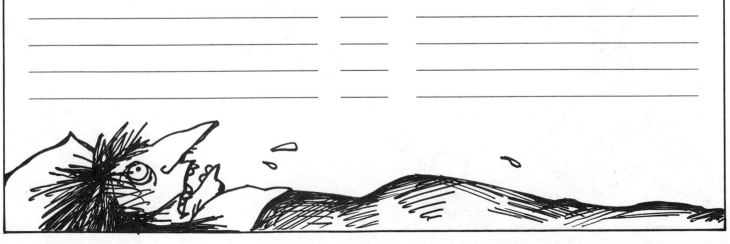

Clue	Answer	Second Clue
Example: a tornado	twister	dot-touching party game
1. pairs		
2. in the middle		
3. little branch pieces		
4. months		
5. 2 x once		
6. thread		
7. car polish		
8. Belgium's chief port		
9. sparkle		
10. bird sound		
11. Samuel Clemens		
12. turnabout dance		
13. plucking tool		
14. *inward's* opposite		
15. baton move		
16. time before dark		
17. multicolored fabric		
18. body spasm		

See if you can create five clues for *sw* words. It is difficult to find *sw* in the middle of any word.

Short-Term Project

Four hot air balloons are pictured below. Complete the questions that follow before designing and naming each of your balloon creations.

1. Your name: _____

2. Your crewmates' names: _____

3. Two destinations to which your balloon will travel: _____

_____

4. Method of pick-up after you've landed: _____

5. Articles your balloon will carry:_____

6. Date of trip: _____ Approximate travel time: _____

7. Key geographical features of areas you will pass: _____

_____

8. Landmarks and historic sites you will pass:_____

_____

9. The country's flag you will be carrying: _____

Ideas and Illustrations

Get a large piece of art paper and divide it into four parts. Thirty "you are" themes are listed below. Pick four of them to illustrate, one in each section of the art paper. You may choose to do a larger mural with a "you are" label on each drawing. Think of a situation that would occur if each "you are" theme was put into practice or actually happened to you. Develop each template into a mini story with accompanying illustrations.

1. You are one of the Twits.
2. You are stuck in mud, head first.
3. You are a hair designer.
4. You are a designer of creative beards and mustaches.
5. You are a bird being chased by a hunter.
6. You are twelve. Your body is completely covered by hair.
7. You are the creator of talking schoolbooks.
8. You are the person who is stuck to a chair with glue.
9. You are a mad scientist who is creating salt that will stick to French fries.
10. You are Father Dirt, the designer of a soap that is guaranteed to remove grime and grease from all fabrics.
11. You are the boyfriend of Mr. Twit's daughter.
12. You are the referee in the championship bout of the World Wrestling Federation.
13. You are a boomerang.
14. You are a baseball bat hitting a game-winning home run.
15. You are a member of the pit crew of a famous racer.
16. You are the world's record holder for pizza eating.
17. You have just participated in a quantum leap to the planet Mars. Show the Earth in contrast to Mars.
18. You are a world champ bubble gum design maker.
19. You are a basketball player's sneaker.
20. You are a famous singer.
21. You are a painting that has people who move.
22. You are lost in a forest of strange trees and animals.
23. You are the discoverer of the *Titanic*.
24. You are being chased by a monster's hand.
25. You are the mother of one of the Seven Dwarfs.
26. You are an Olympic champion.
27. You are a volcano on one of the Hawaiian Islands.
28. You are an old-fashioned car, boat or train.
29. You are a lion watching your pride.
30. You are a criminal wanted for a crime.

71

Student Research Suggestions

1. Survey your class with the question "What do you think are the three worst traits of the Twits?" Make bar, line and circle graphs with your findings.

2. Plan a normal pajama party on one half of an 11" x 14" (27.94 x 35.56 cm) paper. On the other half, design a Twit pajama party contrasting normal happenings with the Twits' way of conducting themselves. Research other party formats (birthday, welcome home, graduation) and illustrate how Twit "weirdness" would have an effect on each celebration.

3. You are a newspaper reporter who is researching people for a *Ripley's Believe It or Not* article. Write the newspaper article (with photo) of how you will feature Mr. or Mrs. Twit. Review two articles in a Ripley's book and try to either follow the same style or go off in new writing directions of your own.

4. Find out what local colleges are conducting animal studies. Write a short paper describing two of the studies. Research the procedures used for allowing animals to be used for study in your state.

5. Recruit a panel discussion for this topic: "We Can Help the Twits." Focus on ways to improve one's appearance and personality. Write a letter to the Twits explaining that your class is doing research on the topic of health and grooming and that you would like them to appear on your panel. Have your class write some questions they'd like to ask each Twit.

6. You are Mr. Twit's best friend. Keep an illustrated diary of two of the happenings from the story from your artistic perspective.

7. Write a science fiction story concerning the intelligence of monkeys and birds. Sprinkle it with enough scientific facts to keep your audience's interest.

8. Research extinct birds. Support your research with illustrations on a mural called "From Dodoes to Flying Dinosaurs."

9. Make a four-part drawing with the theme "The Four Best Friends of Humans." Think beyond animals to things like water, sunshine and liver.

10. Write an "Incredible Mr. Twit" poem or limerick.

11. Write a "Mr. Twit for President" article for *Time* magazine.

12. Draw an expanded map of Mr. Twit's beard.

Teacher Suggestions

1. Designing album, cassette or CD covers combines writing, artistic and photographic talent. Invite a record producer to your school for a classroom demonstration of the process from recording to art studio to record shelves. If one is not available, talk to a local small business owner about who does their packaging. Have the class bring examples of eye-catching and creative packaging. After discussing all these processes, introduce your students to the project of designing an album cover for a new record based on the story about the Twits. Make lists of what should be included before challenging everyone's creativity in album cover design.

2. Have your class design King of the Twits banners and bumper stickers that could be used to advertise the book or movie. Place them on a clothesline near your window for an excellent display.

3. One of the teachers in my school made a bus stop drawing with each character from *The Twits* standing at the bus stop. She then had everyone write and illustrate stories about where the bus should take the Twits. She pinned these writings and drawings to a sheet and hung the sheet up like a giant wall tapestry. It is a real eye-catcher from the second to the seventh grades. This same thing can be done with a giant wall hanging of unusual characters from children's literature. Attach to it writings and drawings of where students would go in search of the Twit family.

4. Have a Let's Welcome the Twits to Our School Day where the children must dress up, draw pictures or make dioramas as close to the scenes and characters in the story as possible. Speeches welcoming each Twit to the school can also be presented by your students. Have your class create "worst awards" that might be presented to the Twits.

5. One of my best friends is a balloonist with many an exciting story and some amazing pictures shot from his balloon. The chasers have just as many interesting stories. Have a local balloonist or club present some of the joys of ballooning to the class.

6. Make suggestions for The Twits Can Be Helped poster contest with your students.

7. Have your students create a diner called The Twits. What strange items would appear on the menu?

8. Organize a What Is a Muggle Wump contest. Have the class bring in real objects and objects that they have designed. Each object should be the student's impression of what a Muggle Wump really is.

9. Make a "top ten" list of things the Twits are most famous for with your students.

10. Organize a class In Search of the Twits expedition. Design explorer hats and T-shirts. Focus your math, social studies, geography, reading, science and literature on this classroom quest. Have the class write Leonard Nimoy's narration. It can be given every half hour to report on the progress of the operation. Step-by-step, illustrated maps can be used for the journey. On their maps the students must pass through two areas that represent other stories from children's literature. Show the class "Rock and Roll Mother Goose" as an example of how many stories can be integrated into one central theme.

GA1459

Write Like a Master

Each of your stories should be centered around something that the reader will say is disgusting. Remember that the disgusting thing that you are writing about must be acceptable in a school setting. Some of the original Grimm's fairy tales were disgusting, like the part in "Cinderella" where mothers cut their children's toes to make their feet fit in the glass slipper. You may want to check with your teacher before writing a final draft of your story, just to make sure none of your details are too disgusting.

Story Starter I

The most disgusting job in our household is having to clean out the cat's litter box. It almost makes me sick. The only job that could be worse is _____

_____

_____

_____

Story Starter II

The glob of toxic waste floated down the river and just seemed to eat or melt everything in sight. The only thing left anywhere was eyeballs! Yes, eyeballs! For some reason the waste did not dissolve eyeballs. The road was _____

_____

_____

_____

Story Starter III

These gloves are the dumbest things. They are designed to prevent me from scratching my chicken pox. I feel like _____

_____

_____

_____

Story Starter IV

Have you ever watched a baby try to eat cake and ice cream? For my little sister's birthday, we gave her a piece of cake and a scoop of chocolate ice cream. Then we all stood back and watched as she_____

_____

_____

_____

Story Starter V

I can't cut up this frog. It was probably someone's pet. _____

_____

_____

_____

GA1459

Public Speaking

Create an outline for a two-minute speech on each of these topics. Write three of your outline categories in the spaces provided. This will help your teacher see that your speech preparation is on the right track.

1. You are giving the speech to introduce Mr. Twit as the winner of The Most Disgusting Man in Children's Literature award. Explain how the award is selected and describe the points that made Mr. Twit the winner.

   Outline Category 1: _____

   Outline Category 2: _____

   Outline Category 3: _____

2. You are a fashion expert who is helping to change Mrs. Twit's appearance. How would you describe her appearance? What ideas do you have for bettering her looks?

   Outline Category 1: _____

   Outline Category 2: _____

   Outline Category 3: _____

3. You are an ornithologist describing your state's bird or the birds in your area. What would your selection include?

   Outline Category 1: _____

   Outline Category 2: _____

   Outline Category 3: _____

4. You are a witch doctor who has this formula that will make disgusting people disappear. What are the key points of your product, and how can it be best used?

   Outline Category 1: _____

   Outline Category 2: _____

   Outline Category 3: _____

5. After picking two of your favorite TV stars, you are to give a speech describing why their marriage is the perfect marriage. Stars' names: _____ _____

   Outline Category 1: _____

   Outline Category 2: _____

   Outline Category 3: _____

6. You are the creator of zoo habitats. You specialize in putting animals in their natural surroundings. Describe three of your most famous habitats.

   Outline Category 1: _____

   Outline Category 2: _____

   Outline Category 3: _____

Write your two-minute speech on the back of this sheet.

GA1459

The Claim Game
States and Capitals

Materials Needed: die, movers and colored crayons

ROAD MAP

Outer trail (top row): AUSTIN · YOUR STATE CAPITAL · AUGUSTA · TRENTON · SALT LAKE CITY · COLUMBUS

Outer trail (left column): BATON ROUGE · HARRIS-BURG · SANTA FE · MADISON · SALEM · HONOLULU · ATLANTA

Outer trail (right column): DES MOINES · LINCOLN · YOUR BORDER STATE'S CAPITAL · ALBANY · CHEYENNE · BOISE · PIERRE

Center region:

MAINE	NEW MEXICO	SOUTH DAKOTA	GEORGIA
WYOMING	IOWA	NEW YORK	WISCON-SIN
YOUR STATE	HAWAII	OREGON	UTAH
NEBRASKA	IDAHO	YOUR BORDER STATE	LOUISI-ANA
TEXAS	PENNSYL-VANIA	NEW JERSEY	OHIO

Play Procedure: Throw die. Highest number places mover anywhere on board. Same person rolls die and moves in either direction on the outside trail. Alternate turns. Claiming four boxes in a row in the center region wins the game.

Basic construction and format for the game can be found on page 63. The object of the game will vary accordingly.

HOT	GLAD	COARSE	WEIRD	WIDER	JOLLY

Hink Pinks/Give a Funny Definition

Create a Hink Pink–rhyming words with a funny defini-tion–by landing on first half and matching second.

MOUSE					SLIM
FAT	QUEEN	COLLIE	GIVER	CURTAIN	MERRY
LIVER	SPIDER	BEET	CAT	HORSE	SWEET
CERTAIN	CHERRY	DAD	ARK	POT	HEAVY
TALL	BEARD	BLENDER	WALL	SHEEP	SLENDER
CHEAP	DRINK	CHEVY	HOUSE	JIM	MEAN

Play Procedure: Throw die. Highest number places mover anywhere on board. Same person rolls die and moves in either direction on the outside trail. Alternate turns. Claiming four boxes in a row in the center region wins the game.

| DARK | | | | | PINK |

Basic construction and format for the game can be found on page 63. The object of the game will vary accordingly.

GA1459

The Wonderful Story of Henry Sugar and Six More

Greed

Casinos

Orphanage

Personality

Playing Cards

Exotic Locales

Large Sums of Money

Lead-Ins to Literature

Science fiction stories often talk about civilizations where the inhabitants can read one another's minds. Did you ever think about having the power to read someone's mind? What do you think it would be like to develop such a power? Would it create a world where it was impossible to cheat or lie? Henry Sugar, the lead character in the story, develops the power to read playing cards by looking at the back of the card. Naturally, this ability will allow him to win large sums of money. All the riches of the world at someone's fingertips can really change a person. Will Henry take the road of greed, or will he use the money to help others? Reading *The Wonderful Story of Henry Sugar and Six More* might answer this question. Then again, it may have nothing to do with the story. Now wouldn't that be a great joke on a class of kids . . . a teacher doing an introduction that had nothing to do with the story that was about to be read.

1. If Henry didn't have the power to read playing cards, he would have to gamble to win money. What are your opinions on gambling? _____
   _____
   _____

2. How do you predict Henry acquires the power to read playing cards? What other powers does he have? _____
   _____
   _____

3. If you could see behind things, how would you use this power? Without cheating, is there any way this power could help you with your schoolwork? _____
   _____
   _____

4. What other strange powers have characters in your stories been given? Make a list of five stories and the powers the lead characters had in each.

   a. _____   _____
   b. _____   _____
   c. _____   _____
   d. _____   _____
   e. _____   _____

5. What book character is your favorite hero/heroine? _____
   _____
   _____

6. Would a child use the power to read someone's mind any differently than an adult? Can you come up with three differences in the way each would approach this problem?

   a. _____
   b. _____
   c. _____

7. On the back of this sheet, draw a picture of two people talking to each other by reading each other's minds rather than speaking words.

                    GA1459

Just the Facts

1. Who is the man that "sees without his eyes"? _____

2. What was Henry's age and marital status? _____

3. Where did Henry make his home?_____

4. What type of car did Henry drive? _____

5. The first three orphanages were established in _____, _____ and _____.

6. Henry asked John Winston to be his money man, banker and _____.

7. Who gave Henry the idea of using his power and wealth to building orphanages? _____

8. John Winston and his staff administered and financed twenty-one orphanages throughout the world. All this was done from Lausanne. What was the company's name? _____

9. Everyone tried to beat the casinos with one type of _____ or another, but John Winston told Henry that it was impossible.

10. Stepping across hot coals without being burned was perfected by the Khan. This is called _____.

11. A true Yogi would never misuse his power for personal fame or fortune. A true Yogi only practices his art in absolute privacy. If he violates these rules, his death would be _____ _____and _____

12. If your whole body leaves the ground and becomes suspended in air during prayer, this is called the power of _____.

13. The finale for Imhrat Khan's act was _____.

14. A blue _____ _____ contained John Cartwright's letter concerning his first meeting with the Imhrat Khan at Bombay General Hospital in December 1934.

15. Henry's whole fate seemed to be decided because he drew the low card before beginning a _____ game.

16. Name three secondary characters in the story.

_____   _____   _____

What Is Your Opinion?

1. Do you think that it is possible to see anything with your eyes covered? One of the characters of *Star Trek: The Next Generation* is blind and uses a sight simulator. How do you think it works?_____

_____

2. What three problems could have prevented Henry from winning money at casinos throughout the world?

   a. _____

   b. _____

   c. _____

3. What changes a person from being greedy to a person who shares everything he or she has with needy orphans? _____

_____

4. Survey your classmates to see how many believe that the things that happen in dreams foretell things that will happen in the future. Record your findings below. Give your opinion of why people feel so strongly about this belief. Can you design three other mind-reading questions to include in your mini survey? Make a prediction of the percentage of children that will respond to each question. Compare your predictions to the final results. _____

_____

_____

5. Do you think it is dishonest for someone to use this kind of power to take money from various casinos? Explain your answer. _____

_____

6. Many people say that strengthening our concentration powers is the key to our success in the future. Do you agree with this statement? Do you think anyone in the world could attain Henry's power if he or she worked at it the same way Henry did?_____

_____

7. What would be the repercussions of casinos finding out that their money was being used to finance orphanages all over the world? List five pros and cons of this discovery.

   a. _____   _____

   b. _____   _____

   c. _____   _____

   d. _____   _____

   e. _____   _____

8. Why would a person who did so much for others want to be anonymous?

_____

9. What events in the story are most likely to happen? Which events were the most outrageous and unbelievable? _____

_____

GA1459

❓ Vocabulary Match Game ❓
Vexing Vocabulary I

Pick a partner to play the Vocabulary Match Game with you. Fourteen categories are given below. You and a partner will predict three words in each category. One of the three words must be from the Henry Sugar story. After you have selected your words privately, you compare work sheets to see how many words are the same. The object is not to fool your partner but to select things that each of you will have in common. Score one point for each match and record your score on the fourth blank under each category. Enter the total score for your work sheet in the space provided.

1. What words would you associate with an orphanage?

   _____ _____ _____ Score: _____

2. Large sums of money can be described by what words?

   _____ _____ _____ Score: _____

3. Places a rich person might visit

   _____ _____ _____ Score: _____

4. Adjectives that will describe Henry's friends

   _____ _____ _____ Score: _____

5. What words could be used to show respect for a Yogi?

   _____ _____ _____ Score: _____

6. Imhrat Khan's book began with these three words:

   _____ _____ _____ Score: _____

7. Henry's will contained what unique thoughts/words?

   _____ _____ _____ Score: _____

8. Things you might find in London would include:

   _____ _____ _____ Score: _____

9. What transportation symbols might appear in this story?

   _____ _____ _____ Score: _____

10. Record three words that would appear in a dream.

    _____ _____ _____ Score: _____

11. A business person might write these words on a notepad.

    _____ _____ _____ Score: _____

12. A person might thank Henry for

    _____ _____ _____ Score: _____

13. A deck of playing cards would have these words:

    _____ _____ _____ Score: _____

14. A clothing store would use these words in an ad:

    _____ _____ _____ Score: _____

    Total: _____

Vexing Vocabulary II

giddy   balcony   casinos   audience
Dr. Marshall   enthusiastic   puzzled   genuine
exalted   bandaged   scrimmage   roulette
impatient   performer   episode   stationary
yogi   volcano   patient   John Winston
champagne   conjurors   billed   ignorance

Choose eight of the vocabulary words above and record the sentence where each appears in the story. Circle the vocabulary word in the sentence and record its page number.

1. _____ Page : _____
2. _____ Page : _____
3. _____ Page : _____
4. _____ Page : _____
5. _____ Page : _____
6. _____ Page : _____
7. _____ Page : _____
8. _____ Page : _____

Choose eight different vocabulary words. List two synonyms next to each. One should come from your knowledge and the other from a thesaurus.

Word	Knowledge	Thesaurus
1.		
2.		
3.		
4.		
5.		
6.		
7.		
8.		

Can you use the remaining eight vocabulary words in four sentences? Each sentence will have two vocabulary words in it.

1. _____
2. _____
3. _____
4. _____

GA1459

Sentence Down the Mountain Puzzle
Drills for Skills

Your mountain climbing, sentence acumen and puzzle-solving abilities will all come into play in this activity. You start with the word at the top of the mountain and try to make a sentence by the time you get to the bottom row of the mountain. All sentences must end with a word on the bottom row. Sentences are formed by leaving one box and entering another box that touches the one you just left. Each time you enter a box, that word must be part of your sentence. As you proceed down the mountain you are trying to form as many sentences as possible. See if you can find five sentences for each mountain on this page. Test your creativity by designing a mountain that will generate more sentences than any mountain your classmates discover.

Example:

	BILL	
ONLY	WANTED	
TRIED	MONEY	BEN

Bill wanted Ben.
Bill only tried money.
Bill only wanted money, Ben.
Bill only wanted Ben.
Bill wanted money.

	I	
AM	CRIED	
SICK	JOHN	TODAY

	THE	
BALL	GAME	
BROKE	ENDED	SOON

	OPEN	
YOUR	MY	
CASE	BOOK	SCHOOL

	SIT	
DOWN	SOON	
SLOWLY	MARK	PLEASE

	WHO	
IS	MET	
MARTIN	SUSAN	YOU

	LOOK	
FOR	YOUR	
KIDS	HAPPY	RIGHT

	NO	
ONE	PERSON	
TRIPPED	WAS	STOPPED

GA1459

Sentence Down the Mountain Puzzle
Drills for Skills Blank Master

Your mountain climbing, sentence acumen and puzzle solving abilities will all come into play in this activity. You start with the word at the top of the mountain and try to make a sentence by the time you get to the bottom row of the mountain. All sentences must end with a word on the bottom row. Sentences are formed by leaving one box and entering another box that touches the one you just left. Each time you enter a box, that word must be part of your sentence. As you proceed down the mountain you are trying to form as many sentences as possible. Test your creativity by designing a mountain that will generate more sentences than any mountain your classmates discover. This blank master has been designed for you to create walk down sentences of your own.

85

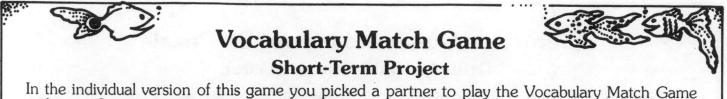

Vocabulary Match Game
Short-Term Project

In the individual version of this game you picked a partner to play the Vocabulary Match Game with you. Categories were given. You and a partner had to predict three words in each category. After each of you had selected your words privately, you compared work sheets to see how many words were the same. The object is not to fool your partner but to select things that each of you will have in common. The classroom form of this game is similar. It is almost like the national game Facts in Five. Your teacher will give the categories, or you can use the ones below. Your first two choices should be predictions as to what most of the students in your class will write. You get one point for each classmate you match. A simple show of hands will allow you to record how many people selected the same word you did. The third word this time is a word you feel only you have thought of in the particular category mentioned. If no one in the class matches your word, you receive ten points. Draw a mini illustration of one of your choices from each round in the art box included with each category.

Topic	Word One	Word Two	Unique Word	Drawing
Space Word				
Tender Words				
Foolish Words				
Fish				
Wild Animals				
Cars				
Games				
Furniture				
Jobs				
Hobbies				

Total: _____

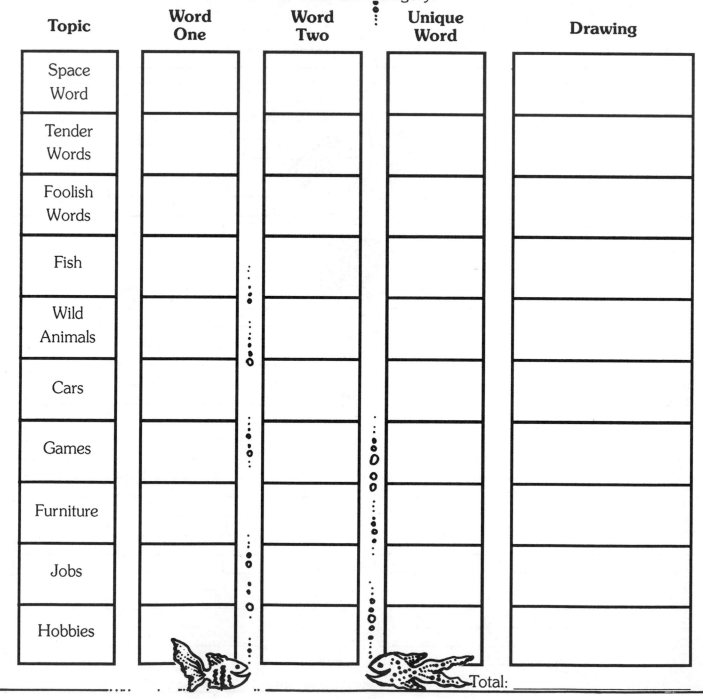

GA1459

Ideas and Illustrations

If you ever attend a lecture on how to open a small business, you will find that a key marketing strategy is to improve something that everyone uses. One of my marketing favorites concerns the woman who took a rock, put it into a creative looking box and called it a "Pet Rock." She then proceeded to convince America that a Pet Rock is what everyone needed. It was less costly than a real pet, didn't make a mess and didn't have to be walked at three in the morning. She made millions of dollars with this idea. The next year she came out with "Rock Stars." This time she glued stars to rocks and sold them everywhere. "Desk Rocks" had the saying "Please turn me over" on one side. When you turned the rock over, it said "Thank you" on the other side. Creative, simple and what everyone needs—a pet, a paperweight, a good laugh.

You are to create or improve a set of playing cards. Six outlines are given below. Rectangular cards may be the easiest to hold, but many of you have probably seen a round deck of cards. Don't let the form given below restrict your ideas for the size and shape of your deck. Design the fronts and backs of the three playing cards below. Mail your class's best ideas to one of the national card manufacturers. You never know. Maybe you'll receive that money your class needs for a new computer.

GA1459

Student Research Suggestions

You are the owner of the most famous orphanage in the world. Your love for and methods of care for children are being studied by everyone from teachers to administrators of foster care programs. You are about to appear on *33-33*, a half-hour news program that features people involved in service to their communities. They have asked you to detail your background, education and creative ideas for child care on the form below. Even though you are upset with having to fill out a form, you give the show's producers a whole spectrum of ideas that will help them produce an outstanding show on your work and creative ideas.

1. What is your name? _____

2. Is this your real name, or are you like Henry Sugar and trying to conceal your identity?_____
   _____

3. Where did you set up your first orphanage, and why did you choose this location? _____
   _____

4. What were your original goals for taking so many children off the streets? _____
   _____
   _____

5. How many children have you placed with permanent families in our area? _____
   _____

6. How do you select the families who will adopt your orphans, and what qualities do you look for in the families you select? _____
   _____

7. Would you ever consider giving a child to a single person? Why doesn't this happen more often in our child care system? _____
   _____

8. Where does most of the funding for your orphanages originate? _____
   _____

9. The children in your orphanages seem so happy, well fed and well educated. Explain the model you use in your orphanages. _____
   _____

10. A great many of your staff members were orphans whom you placed in homes and jobs and came back to help you continue your work. What do you attribute this fact to? _____
    _____
    _____

Draw a diagram of one of your orphanages on the back of this sheet.

GA1459

Teacher Suggestions

1. Make a classroom mural titled "Henry's Orphanages." Have your class draw mini pictures of orphanage buildings. Then take a large map of the world and mount the orphanages at key locations. Each student should then write a brief description of the orphanage's locale. Place these write-ups around the map. Take white or colored string and run it from the orphanage on the map to its write-up outside the map. Design an index key to place next to the map.

2. Contact your local police station and arrange for a class visit by a person responsible for finding lost children. Have him or her discuss the new child identification program that is now being enacted in locations around the United States.

3. Have your class design a virtual reality video game. The theme should be Famous Humanitarians. Discuss what a humanitarian is and then present examples of some of the more famous (Schweitzer, St. Theresa, Nobel, Pulitzer). The machine should be designed so the game player is actually in the life of the person that is highlighted.

4. Research America's Animal Refuges and compare the programs we offer for animals to those we have for abandoned or foster children.

5. Discuss and show examples of famous buildings to your students. Have them analyze what the architect is trying to express, or have your class determine the most outstanding feature of the buildings that you show them. Have them select styles that might be used in one of Henry's orphanages. Architecture collages can then be made. Pieces from five buildings or structures should be cut out and then formed into one building. The effect this produces is akin to abstract architecture.

6. Gambling is a very delicate subject. Make a list of all the gambling options in your area. It is shocking how many you will find, from bingo to the state lotteries to horse racing. Philadelphia is one hour away from Atlantic City, but there are no awareness programs offered for young children in the area. This addiction can destroy a family just as quickly as drugs or alcohol. Many people have jobs in this industry, so it is important to present the positive aspects of this industry while making children aware that gambling isn't as glamorous as it looks.

7. Divide the class in half. One half of the class collects phrases that have to do with winning a big prize, lottery or clearinghouse sweepstakes, while the other half collects phrases that have to do with being disappointed.

8. Have a Bring an Imaginary Mentor to School Day. Draw and describe imaginary mentors to classmates. These mentors are sponsoring the children the same way kings and queens sponsored artists years ago. Children describe the areas they are being sponsored in, as well as exhibiting their best works so far in those areas.

9. What type of company would be consulted to design an orphanage? Are there any architectural offices or colleges near your school? Design a thinking web with your class showing all the industries connected with building and financing an orphanage or casino.

Write Like a Master

Complete the story starters below using the theme that some fortune-telling or mind-reading problem is growing out of proportion. Try to incorporate some scientific facts into each story. Give the reader the feeling that the unexplained will soon be happening again.

Story Starter I

I know he read my mind. While he was staring at me, I could feel my mind being drained. The times tables that I knew yesterday just seemed to disappear from my brain. I had trouble remembering some of my favorites like chocolate chip cookies, ice cream and Billy Riggins. If he is trying to find out things about me, I may lose those ideas that are important to me. Who can I turn to? If I am wrong, _____

_____

_____

_____

Story Starter II

It is my favorite radio show. I just love it when the announcer says, "And now turn your mind over to Ultron, master of impossible dreams." Each week the show introduces_____

_____

_____

_____

Story Starter III

Did you ever have a day where your mind was two answers beyond the questions that were being asked? You know the kind of day I am talking about . . . a "perfect, everything-goes-right" day. The last time that happened to me was_____

_____

_____

_____

Story Starter IV

Buy Thinkit–the greatest chewing gum since Home Run Power. All your thinking problems will be solved on the first chew. Pop a piece in your mouth before your next math or spelling test and "presto"! You will_____

_____

_____

_____

Story Starter V

Welcome to the home of the Great Renardo, fortune-teller to the stars. My predictions for good fortune, business success, and sometimes even love are world famous. I have read your cards and stars. I have found _____

_____

_____

GA1459

Public Speaking

You are a student or teacher who is giving a two-minute speech to a local elementary, high school or college class. Your supervisor wants to see your notes before you give your speech. Record three of your top points for each speech choice on the lines below each topic. Then write a mini presentation for the speech topic you feel best qualified to introduce.

1. You are speaking on behalf of a local orphanage. It is their annual fund drive. This year they need money for a new dormitory and gym. You are requesting help with the drive, as well as contributions for the building fund. _____

_____

_____

2. The world famous Oracle of Delphi is speaking to your teaching group. What three questions would you ask her about her powers to tell the future? If you were introducing her to this group, what accomplishments of hers would you feature in your speech? _____

_____

_____

3. A rock and roll group is performing at your school. The name of the group is The Mystics. How would you introduce them? _____

_____

_____

4. You are a flight attendant who is describing the religious temples deep in India's mountain regions. _____

_____

_____

5. You want to study with a famous wise person, who is now sitting in front of you with legs crossed asking you why you have traveled so far to pursue your dream. This wise person also wants to know what sacrifices you have made to become a better student. What explanation will you give? _____

_____

_____

6. Campers are needed for your school camping trip. _____

_____

_____

7. You have invented a new card game. _____

_____

_____

8. Dogs from a local animal shelter need families to adopt them. _____

_____

GO BACK TO START	ABLE	DONATION	PLAN	LONDON	SPELL A VOCABULARY WORD
STORM					GREED
UNICORN	1	3	2	3	FIERCE
REMAIN	3	2	1	2	OHIO
BLAME	3	1	2	3	ODOR
IDAHO	1	2	3	1	STRENGTH
FRIEND	2	3	1	2	TOUR
PLEASE					FENDER
START	PREDICT	IOWA	YOGI	AROMA	LOSE A TURN

Syllable Search

Move on the outside trail. Cover up or color in the number of syllables in the word you land on. A box of four of your markers or colored-in boxes in the inner region wins.

A total of twenty-five syllables also wins. Alternate turns with a partner. This same game can be played with a pile of vocabulary cards and the gameboard center.

Basic construction and format for the game can be found on page 63. The object of the game will vary accordingly.

GA1459

GO BACK TO START

SPELL A VOCABULARY WORD

Syllable Search
Blank Student Gameboard

1	2	3	4
4	1	2	3
3	4	1	2
2	3	4	1
1	2	3	4

Use the vocabulary from the Henry Sugar story. Words from any subject you are studying can be placed around the gameboard. States, capitals, famous people or classmates' names can also be used.

START

LOSE A TURN

Basic construction and format for the game can be found on page 63. The object of the game will vary accordingly.

GA1459

George's Marvelous Medicine

Lead-Ins to Literature

Most stories make grandmothers and grandfathers cute, lovable and helpful people, especially when the grandchildren are nearby. Too bad this story isn't the same! How does "not even close" sound to you? Before reading this story please remember that the grandmother in this book is pure fiction. She is somebody created by a wild pen. She was designed to make you laugh, I think. Is she a wizard or just an "old cranky?" Will George's medicine protect him and cure her or will . . . never mind, just read the story.

1. Can you think of any other stories that feature a child's grandparents?_____
   _____
   _____

2. You are an author of a story that makes fun of grandparents. What three things that grand-parents do would you highlight and make fun of in your writing?

   a._____
   b._____
   c._____

3. Grandmother has animals all over the place. What animals, would you guess, fit into a story of a cranky grandmother and a secret medicine? Why did you choose the animals that you did? Explain. _____
   _____
   _____

4. Record three descriptive words and one statement about a grandmother, and then see if these words or your statement appeared in the story. _____
   _____
   _____

5. What should young children know about medicine and who is responsible for teaching them?
   _____
   _____

6. George is going to make a mixture of things to help his grandmother. What common house-hold liquids would be dangerous if mixed together or used alone? _____
   _____
   _____

7. Construction machinery plays a humorous role in this story. List three guesses as to the type of machinery that will be featured in this book. _____
   _____
   _____

8. Size plays an important part in George's tale. Would large things or small things get more laughs? Why? _____
   _____

Just the Facts

Determine which facts below are true and which are false. Rewrite each false fact on the line below the statement. If the fact is true, describe its relationship to the story on the lines below the statement.

1. Blue paint was the key to the secret mixture. _____ T F

_____

_____

2. George's brother and sister did not live at home. _____ T F

_____

3. Grandma slept in the barn and was as frisky as a cat. _____ T F

_____

4. Six-foot-long chicken necks make good eating. _____ T F

_____

5. The black cockerel amazed Mr. Billy Kranky. _____ T F

_____

6. 11:20 was a good time for Grandma's medicine. _____ T F

_____

7. Fifty doses of medicine was too much for Grandma. _____ T F

_____

8. Grandma used Brillident to clean her teeth. _____ T F

_____

9. The bedroom supplied George with mixture supers. _____ T F

_____

10. Grandma's powers twisted creatures in weird shapes. _____ T F

_____

11. Slugs will definitely make cabbage taste good. _____ T F

_____

12. Growing is a nasty habit in George's opinion. _____ T F

_____

13. Watching Grandma on Sunday was a drag for George. _____ T F

_____

14. George was forbidden to touch Grandma's perfume. _____ T F

_____

15. George carried the soup pot through the house. _____ T F

_____

What Is Your Opinion?

1. Fooling around with things in the medicine cabinet, as well as mixing all sorts of household liquids in a pot, is dangerous. Why would an author put such things in a story? Wouldn't he be afraid that children would immediately go out and imitate the dangerous mixtures mentioned in the story? _____

   _____

2. Grandma's ticks and fleas bothered me the most. What characteristic of Grandma's would you classify as her worst? _____

   _____

3. Grandma never told George what would happen if an eight-year-old boy didn't stop growing. What goofy antigrowing reasons would you write to make her seem even crazier? _____

   _____

4. The chicken on stilts was my choice for funniest animal in the story. What would your choice be? Explain why. _____

   _____

5. If this story was the first Roald Dahl story that you read, how would you describe the author? Would you want to read another book by Roald Dahl? Explain why or why not. _____

   _____

6. If you had a choice of being extremely tall or extremely small, which one would you select? What would be the benefits of either choice? _____

   _____

7. What one medicine is the most important one in your medicine cabinet? What are its benefits/dangers? _____

   _____

8. Do you think the author saw *Honey, I Shrunk the Kids* before writing this story of the incredible shrinking grandmother? What was similar about the stories? _____

   _____

9. Enormous animals could be the solution to the world's hunger problems. How would you suggest that George's formula be duplicated? Brown paint? You must be kidding! _____

   _____

10. List three other options George could have used to change his grandmother instead of the secret mixtures. _____

Vexing Vocabulary

One of the goals of the vocabulary sections in this book is to make you aware of the important words in each story. A second goal is to teach you how to train yourself in recording and studying words you don't know or should know. You should begin keeping a word journal for each book that you read. Word journals organized by category look professional. The word journal below has been started for you. Add three words to each category from *George's Marvelous Medicine* or from your own experience. Add four additional categories and five words from each to represent Grandma and George's family in your journal. Share your list with a classmate.

Cranes	**Medicine**	**Farmyard**	**The Mixture**
vehicle	potion	fence post	stir
hoist	wafer	enormous	fiery
loading	greedy	bullocks	slugs
axle	polish	cockerel	cabbage
puncture	mustard	blender	teaspoon
load	peppercorns	marmalade	colossal
spare	brutal	somersault	nostrils

My four *George's* categories and words are as follows:

1. _____   2. _____   3. _____   4. _____

Did you ever keep a journal of characters in your readings? People in the news? Sports figures? Explorers? Make believe you are George's somewhat crazy grandmother. Keep a diary of her thoughts for a week. Bring them in to share with your classmates. Illustrate her funniest day.

Keep a journal as a shrunken person. Describe all the ways you've had to adjust to your surroundings.

Write a mini journal titled "A Chicken's Life Isn't Much to Cluck About."

Ask your post office or police station for a missing person's poster. Then make a missing person's poster requesting the whereabouts of George's grandmother. Try incorporating the book's vocabulary in your poster. Find out about the National Missing Children Hotline in your city or state.

Triangular Words
Drills for Skills

Triangular words are progressive (each word has one more letter than the previous word). Because of this, they appear to form the shape of a triangle. Each word adds one new letter to the letters in the word below it.

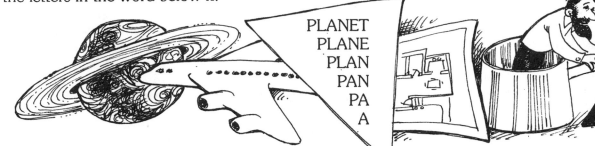

PLANET
PLANE
PLAN
PAN
PA
A

See if you can design three word triangles of your own.

Triangular poems start with one word and progress so that each line has one more word. The words need not be the same. You may use a rhyme form if you desire.

School.
Learning place.
Gain enough knowledge.
Illiteracy you will erase.
Help yourself and a friend.
Many people find education without end.

Try a triangular poem and experiment with a rhyme form of your own.

_____

_____

_____

_____

_____

_____

_____

_____

_____

The Eight-Number Problems
Short-Term Project

Answer: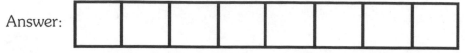

Place these numbers in the boxes above: 1, 1, 2, 2, 3, 3, 4, 4. The ones should be separated by one box; the twos are separated by two boxes; the threes by three; the fours by four boxes. Practice in the box below before putting your work in the answer boxes.

Place the numbers 1, 2, 3, 4, 5, 6, 7 and 8 in the boxes below so no two consecutive numbers touch at any point.

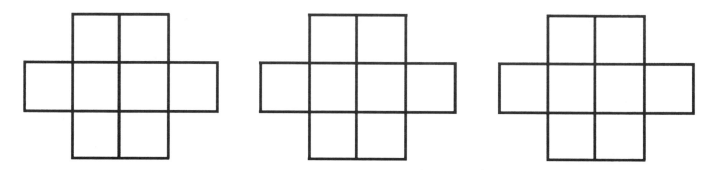

If you are having difficulty, try making cutout numbers for these problems or use the work sheet on the following page.

GA1459

The Eight-Number Problems Work Sheet
Short-Term Project

If you are having difficulty with the Eight-Number Problem puzzles, cut out the numbers below and experiment with moving them to various locations until you have the answers for both problems.

101

Write Like a Master

The theme of the story starters below is a mystery formula or potion that has unknown and mystical powers. Review some of the old mixtures, from Merlin's secret potion to C.S. Lewis' healing potion in *The Lion, the Witch and the Wardrobe*.

Story Starter I

This is the ultimate cure-all. Anytime something bad is about to happen, rub this cream on the bridge of your nose and your troubles will vanish. It cures the common cold and warts, to name a few of its many uses. Last week, the most improbable thing happened. The formula_____

_____

_____

_____

Story Starter II

John felt really strange after swallowing that spoonful of medicine. His hearing seemed to decrease while his vision seemed to improve greatly. He looked at the bottle's label . . . .Good and Bad was a strange name for a medicine. What was even stranger is what happened next. His hair _____

_____

_____

Story Starter III

Welcome to Bottletron, the Nintendo™ of the next century. Pick your game pill, pop it in your mouth, put on the ultimate reality helmet and, presto, you will be transported into a world of

_____

_____

_____

Story Starter IV

The formula is this close to being ready. One more ingredient and Mr. Penniless will finally be able to put food on the table for his family. Changing parents' tears to smiles of joy, if it works, will be much more rewarding than any dollar amount that it will bring. Tomorrow _____

_____

_____

_____

Story Starter V

You disappear for exactly one minute after biting into this pill. The fun you can have will keep you laughing for a week. Yesterday, I took a bite while I was in _____

_____

_____

GA1459

Ideas and Illustrations

You are the head of a pharmaceutical company's packaging division. A new product is just about to come on the market. You are responsible for designing a pill shape, wafer shape, bottle, cream tube and poster for this new product. Fill in the information on the blanks below before completing your drawings.

Your name: _____

Your company's name: _____

City of main office: _____

Type of room used for your work (office, studio etc.): _____

Name of the new product: _____

Product uses: _____

Target audience: _____

Your advertising campaign's theme and structure: _____

Pill	Poster
Bottle	
Cream Tube	
Wafer	

Student Research Suggestions

In the story when George's grandmother was too large to move around, a construction crane was used. The author did not mention where the crane was rented nor did he mention the crane's cost. You are the gaffer for a movie production company and are responsible for getting things for the movie *George's Marvelous Medicine*. The producer wants to see where you purchased items for the movie and how much they cost. Search area stores for the following items. Then compare your research list with your classmates' to find the cheapest location for each prop needed for the movie.

Item	Store Name	Purchase Price	Rental Price
Crane			
Limousine			
Bottle of aspirin			
Bottle of Advil™			
Gallon of brown paint			
Ham/eggs breakfast			
Haircuts for women			
Haircuts for men			
Roof repair (20' x 20')			
5-pound turkey			
Hour pony ride			
Full day horse carriage ride			
Baby-sitting for one hour			
Your item			
Your item			

Attach coupons for reduced prices to this sheet.

GA1459

Student/Teacher Suggestions

1. George is sometimes frightened by his grandmother. Write the dialogue that would be spoken between George and his grandmother as she was being picked up by the crane. Maybe you can have George assuring her that it will not hurt.

2. Write a letter to a crane rental company asking for:
   a. company background/customer profile
   b. types of cranes available
   c. licenses needed
   d. company logos and patches
   e. company hats and stickers
   f. company employees who will talk to your class
   g. trip availability at local facility or school yard demonstration
   h. ways computers/art are used in their business
   i. machine maintenance information

3. Grandparents are often taken for granted. Research national Grandparents' Day; then organize a Grandparents' Day in your school or classroom.
   a. Design a symbol representing the respect and the positive effect grandparents provide at home.
   b. Research activities available for senior citizens in your community.
   c. Check your school system to find out what it is doing in intergenerational studies.

4. Research stories where the children visit or interact with grandparents or other senior citizens.

5. Make a top ten list of books and authors that feature older citizens. 1991 and 1992 were excellent years for books with these themes.

6. Have a covered-dish luncheon where each child brings an imaginary cutout grandmother or grandfather. Each child introduces the imaginary grandparent and explains the relationship, as well as likes and dislikes.

7. Visit a community center for older people and research the information that is displayed on their "What Is Going on in the Community" bulletin boards. Conduct an interview with a senior citizen.

8. Set up a tutoring or shadowing program with senior citizens in your neighborhood. You might want to arrange for each child who has failed a grade to get an extra grandperson. Weekly calls, homework checks and in-class tutoring should all be part of the program.

Public Speaking

Many speakers memorize their speeches before giving them. Some speakers put down key words to jog their memories while giving their speeches. List fifteen key words for each speech topic below. These words should jog your memory while giving your speech. Hand them to your teacher before presenting a one-minute speech on one of the following topics:

1. You are a doctor introducing one of your new findings to the American Medical Association. Look at a medical journal before presenting your speech. Describe some of the studies that appear in the journal to your classmates. Give your classmates some indication of the prestige that you have attained from appearing in this world-known journal.

   _____

   _____

2. You have been invited to speak at a retirement home. The home wants suggestions for things that their members can do to become more active. What would you suggest?

   _____

   _____

3. You are a construction crane operator who is sitting with a group of workers at lunchtime. You are sharing some of your most outrageous construction stories and experiences.

   _____

   _____

4. A travel agency has asked you to represent their cruise line at a travel convention. Your audience seems to be a little older than expected. How would you interest them in the activities on your cruise and in the islands you are going to visit? Some people use the ocean liner for their sleeping quarters, others may want to stay on the island. Account for both groups in your speech.

   _____

   _____

5. Years ago everyone used hair tonic. Very few people use it today. Your company wants to revive their hair tonic business. They've asked you to address your classmates on the benefits of their tonic. Design a hair tonic container and use it in your speech.

   _____

   _____

6. You work for a book of world records. You are describing the skinniest person for the skinniest person category. Illustrations and cutouts are a speech must.

   _____

   _____

7. You are the detective who is asked to find Grandmother. Present your investigation and your findings to your classmates.

   _____

   _____

GA1459

GO BACK TO START				SPELL A VOCABULARY WORD

George's Marvelous Medicine

Throw your die before moving around the gameboard. Land on a picture, cover up a word that rhymes with it from the

log	brain	noise	Mike
grouch	boil	pup	dish
tilts	mat	moose	stamp
steam	cheer	Tony	press
fled	begs	still	fig

middle. If you don't have tons of markers, color on the correct middle square. The person that colors the last square wins. You can move in any direction at anytime.

START				LOSE A TURN

Basic construction and format for the game can be found on page 63. The object of the game will vary accordingly.

GA1459

Matilda

GA1459

Lead-Ins to Literature

Most parents brag about their children again and again and again. No matter what their child's faults are, very few parents believe their children could be anything but outstanding. Matilda is outstanding, but her parents don't even know she is alive. Do you think your parents would notice that you were reading adult books at age four and talking meaningful sentences with unique ideas at the age of $1\frac{1}{2}$? Maybe yours but not Matilda's parents! Her dad even tells her she should spend more time watching TV than reading stupid, old books. Does it sound like a super place to live? Not in Matilda's mind! Not only does she have to change things at home, but her favorite teacher also needs some rescuing.

1. When you heard the title *Matilda,* did you think you were going to read a book about an old-fashioned woman or a young girl? Explain. _____

_____

_____

2. Have you read any books about young children with outstanding intelligence? Who were the children and what traits of theirs were special? _____

_____

_____

3. Books showing outstanding intelligence of children that I have read are _____

_____

_____

4. What famous children have you talked about in class or discussed at home? Are there young children in your family or neighborhood that have outstanding ideas? How have you judged their ideas? _____

_____

_____

5. For a week keep a notebook of the best ideas that students in your class have generated or shared or presented. Record the best ideas below.

_____

_____

_____

_____

_____

6. Matilda's dad is a used car salesman. What kind of situations can you predict will happen with his used car lot in the story? Draw a picture of the lot on the back of this sheet.

_____

_____

_____

Just the Facts

1. What was the only book that Matilda had in her house? _____

2. Matilda messed up what part of her dad's body? _____

3. How did Matilda's dad hide gear problems in the used cars that he sold in his lot? _____

4. In what book did Matilda find Old Miss Havisham? _____

5. Miss Trunchbull often wore a belted smock and _____ breeches.

6. Matilda stated that "she didn't know how far that she could go with the _____ tables."

7. What did Miss Trunchbull do with the girl that she grabbed by the pigtails? _____

8. What kind of creature landed in the water glass? _____

9. Who started the newt prank? _____

10. What did Matilda do with the power of her eyes? _____

11. Michael was expected to join his father in the _____ business.

12. A child that shows amazing intelligence is called a _____ child.

13. What color was Dad's Oil of Violets hair tonic? _____

14. Where was the destination of Matilda's family's suitcase packing? _____

15. What teacher was featured in the story? _____

16. Dad didn't want to miss his _____

Please write two facts about the subjects below.

Mrs. Phelps _____

_____

Fred _____

_____

Charles Dickens _____

_____

Ernest Hemingway _____

_____

Superglue _____

_____

Moving chalk _____

_____

Your choice _____

110

What Is Your Opinion?

1. What is the hardest part of being a very young child who is totally neglected by her parents?

_____

2. Would you find it easier telling both parents at once that you are not moving with them or one at a time? Would you ask your brother to support you in not going, or would you let him leave with your family?

_____

3. If you went to school only one month a year, what month would you pick for your schooling? Explain the significance of picking that month.

_____

4. If you bought a talking bird, what words would you teach it? What comical situation can you design for your bird's speech?

_____

5. What is your opinion of telling a child to watch more television instead of reading?

_____

6. Do you think it is appropriate to punish your child by ripping up her library book and then making her pay for it out of the money that she has earned? Explain your answer.

_____

7. If Matilda had a grandmother or grandfather, would things have been any different in her life? Explain.

_____

8. Should children with great potential be placed in special programs with other children who have the same talents? Why or why not?

_____

9. Has any teacher in your life had the same effect on you that Miss Honey had on Matilda?

_____

10. Why do you think Roald Dahl named his teacher Miss Honey? Was he using the name to make fun of sweet teachers?

_____

11. Matilda's dad's cheating on the car lot was horrible. Which one of his techniques was most upsetting to you? Do you think any of his techniques were dangerous? Why or why not?

_____

12. How would the story have changed if the librarian was not as understanding as Mrs. Phelps was?

_____

Overlapping Sentences
Vexing Vocabulary

splendid   invisible   superglue   shrugged
handle   escape   ridiculous   platinum
phenomenon   liar   lightning   brim
aluminum   sausage   headmistress   murmur
expectations   nightmare   Julius   vast
method   ignorant   expel   halibut

Here is another idea for your vexing vocabulary hall of fame notebook. Each of these sentences will give you a secret message, if you can figure out the key to the code. In each instance, at least one of your vocabulary words is used. Can you decode each sentence on the line provided?

Example: The wide hat *brimproved* her appearance.
The wide hat *brim improved* her appearance.

1. That was a splendidea. _____

2. The liarranged the story so everyone would believe it. _____

3. That is a ridiculouse of invisiblead. _____

4. The murmurgently requested that we close the curtains. _____

5. Do you really believe that I can escapeter's long reach? _____

6. The strange methoddly was one of the most successful of all those that we tested. _____

_____

7. The nightmareturned again last night. A platinumbrella was hiding a strange creature. The creature seemed to have a vastore of energy created from lightning. _____

_____

_____

Can you create five "overlapping word" sentences of your own?

1. _____

2. _____

3. _____

4. _____

5. _____

GA1459

Splendid Words
Drills for Skills

A "splendid word" or homograph is a word that has many meanings. Place three situations for word use under each of the headings below. Try to think of ways to use these words that most people won't think of using.

Most people would put *train your dog* under the train heading below, but a more original idea might be *to train one's mind*.

Homograph	Definition	Definition	Definition	Illustration
Train				
Draw				
Run				
Skip				
Pass				

Place a different definition for each word. Then pick your best definition of the three to illustrate.

Ideas and Illustrations

1. Draw a scene from *Matilda* on board A. Describe the scene on board B.
2. Design a "what is missing from the picture" on board A. Have a classmate record the mistakes on board B.
3. Design a *Matilda* movie on board A and a book poster on board B.

Bar Rows Spelling
Short-Term Project I

Here are two ways to use the chart below.

1. Place a counter on each of the digits in the number your teacher calls out. Does it make a word?
2. Find a word. Place your chips on it. Call out your word's value. See if your classmates can discover it.
   (Example: NONE = 4000 + 400 + 50 + 7 = 4457.)

Teacher Hint: Four see-through bingo markers work best with this project. Call out practice words before starting your class on the project sheet that follows. Each small box is for a change of decimal point if you work with upper grades.

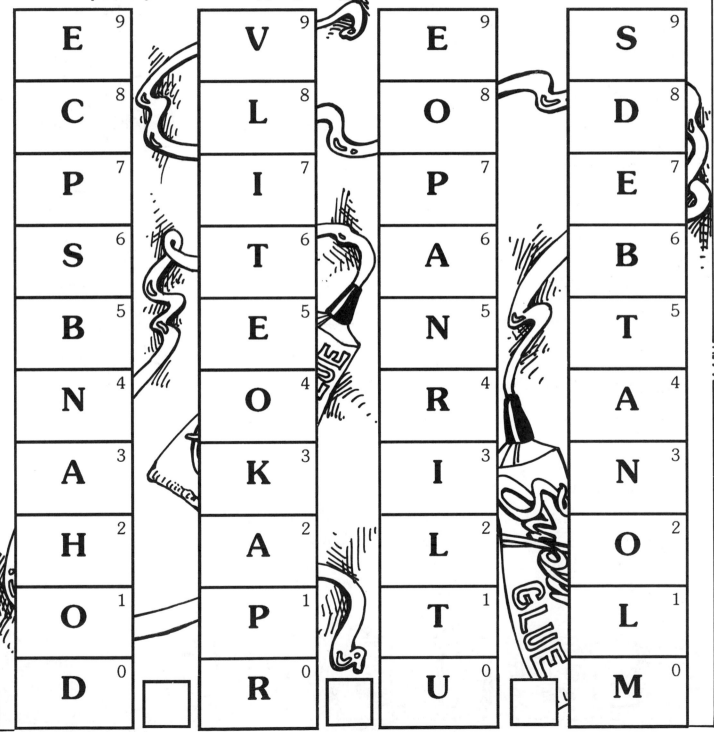

E 9	V 9	E 9	S 9
C 8	L 8	O 8	D 8
P 7	I 7	P 7	E 7
S 6	T 6	A 6	B 6
B 5	E 5	N 5	T 5
N 4	O 4	R 4	A 4
A 3	K 3	I 3	N 3
H 2	A 2	L 2	O 2
O 1	P 1	T 1	L 1
D 0	R 0	U 0	M 0

Bar Rows Spelling
Short-Term Project I
Project Sheet

I. Write the value of each of these words in expanded notation.

1. ball =
2. plan =
3. ore =
4. dine =
5. Stan =

6. ant =
7. tea =
8. put =
9. brim =
10. eat =

II. What words are at these locations?

Example: 5 x 7 = it

a. 2 x 6 =
b. (8 x 8) + 1 =
c. (10 x 10) + 3 =
d. (8 x 9) - 4 =
e. 3 x 11 =

f. 168 + 279 =
g. 387 + 576 =
h. (12 x 12) + 41 =
i. 400 - 173 =
*j. 3 x 3 =

III. What is the largest valued word that starts with each of these letters?

1. N =
2. O =
3. S =

4. K =
5. A =
6. E =

IV. Can you find three contractions and their values?

1.   2.   3.

V. Where are the opposites of these words found?

1. closed _____   * 2. continue _____

VI. Find the value for:

1. a vegetable _____
2. name _____
3. a tree _____
4. a math word _____
5. a gift _____

6. an animal _____
7. clothing _____
8. a school subject _____
9. a drink _____
10. a color _____

Short-Term Project II

Matilda talks about report cards where teachers really get to say what they mean about the children they teach. This could never happen, but let's have some fun thinking up statements that would really describe the work some children may be doing in class. See if you can follow each semi-insulting comment with two of your own. Review the first few pages of *Matilda* to see what Roald Dahl said about "from being a grub to a washout." Go for it! Try to add as much intelligence to your remarks as possible.

Subject: English
Comment: Shakespeare wrote his first sentence at age five.
Your fifteen-year-old son is ten years behind Shakespeare.
Your first:_____
Your second: _____

Subject: Art
Comment: Your child's artwork made Van Gogh cut off his ear.
Your first:_____
Your second: _____

Subject: Math
Comment: Don't *count* on your child passing math, because he can't.
Your first:_____
Your second: _____

Subject: Science
Comment: Minute describes the time humans have spent on earth and the amount of science your child has retained this year.
Your first:_____
Your second: _____

Subject: Computer Science
Comment: Your child's mental files must have been mistakenly deleted in our first disk-saving lesson.
Your first:_____
Your second: _____

Subject: Literature
Comment: Your child enjoyed Poe and the raven that was often on his shoulder. Too bad there's nothing on your child's shoulders or Your child is the Headless Horseman of the sixth grade.
Your first:_____
Your second: _____

Write Like a Master

The theme for the story starters below is the relationship between a child and her favorite teacher. What kind of conversation topics would you select to include in your writing? Will you write both sides of the conversation or write one side? Try to imagine the situations where a teacher and student might have time for personal conversation. Add your own topic to this writing activity.

Story Starter I

Have you talked to your parents about that _____ (boy or girl's name)? I can give you my thoughts, but your parents' ideas come first. It isn't often that someone wants to _____

_____

_____

_____

Story Starter II

This has never happened before! You know what I mean, my teacher wanting to see me after school. It has to be for one of three reasons. Two of the three are bad. How could she know about _____

_____

_____

_____

Story Starter III

Miss Parker, I really enjoyed myself today. You seemed to bring my favorite subject, _____ (insert subject), to life. No, I am not trying to get on your good side with this flattery. I just thought you'd like to know most of the kids in the class like the way _____

_____

_____

_____

Story Starter IV

Quit following me. You are worse than superglue! Everytime I turn around, you are there. It is getting scary! You're not one of those creatures that can change form and move all over the place, are you? That is your secret! The only student that _____

_____

_____

Story Starter V

Here are the five reasons that I will not be allowed to take tests anymore this year in your classroom, Mr. Smith:

1. _____

2. _____

3. _____

4. _____

5. _____

Student Research Suggestions

Your dictionary research techniques will improve after playing the Dictionary Game. In the game you are predicting that your writing is so good no one can figure which definition is the real one and which one is the fake. First, you have to look up a word in the dictionary that you are certain no one in the class knows. Then you are to invent two make-believe definitions for the word. Write the two made-up definitions and the real definition in the blanks provided. Find a competitor to exchange lists with. Score ten points for each word you fool your partner on. If each of you mark your choices on a separate sheet, you can exchange your sheet with a number of different classmates. If you are a good artist, choose your best word and try illustrating the three choices with the written definitions underneath before your challenger makes his or her choice.

Check the definition that you think is correct.

Dictionary word: MAW
Definition 1: Southern slang for *mother*
Definition 2: a stomach
Definition 3: a South American bird
Dictionary word: _____
Definition 1: _____
Definition 2: _____
Definition 3: _____
Dictionary word: _____
Definition 1: _____
Definition 2: _____
Definition 3: _____
Dictionary word: _____
Definition 1: _____
Definition 2: _____
Definition 3: _____
Dictionary word: _____
Definition 1: _____
Definition 2: _____
Definition 3: _____
Dictionary word: _____
Definition 1: _____
Definition 2: _____
Definition 3: _____
Dictionary word: _____
Definition 1: _____
Definition 2: _____
Definition 3: _____
Dictionary word: _____
Definition 1: _____
Definition 2: _____
Definition 3: _____

Record your score. If you didn't fool your partner on many, maybe it is time to review your writing technique. _____

Teacher Suggestions

1. In terms of creativity, one of the most boring school objects is the report card. Discuss the form, format and function of a report card before having your class design report cards that are a little more creative. One of the best suggestions from my class was that the form have a student comment section where students could write how they felt about their own work in each area.

2. Matilda's reading list was quite impressive but maybe out of the reach of most good students. Have your pupils select the ten books that should be on every good reader's list. Have them make title and picture collages to support their opinions.

3. Have a car mechanic visit your class for a "hints that everyone should know about a car" session. After you teach some automotive prerequisites, have your students prepare some questions for your guest.

4. Create a Name is like the occupation list. Your students should list ten names that appear well-suited for their occupations. Some gems from my room included Miss Honey/beekeeper; John Hamilton/sandwich maker; Cheryl Burger (one of our teachers)/hamburger maker; Mary Weaton/cereal maker; Susan Blaw/attorney; Bill Blumenfield/flower shop owner; Lillian Dischinger/plate designer. Most of my class had more success finding occupations for their own names than creating imaginary names that relate to jobs.

5. After discussing the difference in techniques for selling new and used items, have your class design illustrated signs that may appear on a used car lot. This might be a good time to have someone in the collectibles business come in and explain how something used could possibly cost more than something new.

6. Have your class design the floor plans for a children's library. Then in a separate activity, have them name various sections of the library after book characters. The Judy Blume Plant Section was my favorite. Some other examples given by students included Ramona's Records, Peter Pan's Periodicals, Charlotte's Checkout, etc.

7. Have your class design T-shirts announcing deals and specials at Matilda's dad's used car lot.

8. Organize a "children should stay with their parents" debate after a discussion of Matilda's options.

9. Have a Matilda doubling contest. It is organized just like a spelling bee, but numbers and math equations that have to be doubled are used instead of words.

10. Make up five good sayings that show the bad side of cheating (winners never cheat; cheaters never win).

Public Speaking

Here are some speaking topics that coordinate with the story *Matilda*. You have a minute and a half to talk on the topics below. Use the lines provided for some brief points that your teacher may review to see that your ideas are heading in the right direction before you give your talk. Please use the back of this paper to expand your thoughts.

1. You are a teacher that has to tell two parents that their child is being left behind in school this year. Do you think the speech would be different if you were talking about a younger or older student? Explain both situations to your classmates before starting your talk.

2. You are a child who realizes that your parents better hear about your failing schoolwork from you before the school notifies them. Discuss two possible strategies for your speech before starting the one you will present.

3. Matilda's dad is a dishonest car salesman who continually brags about cheating people. How would you convince him in a child-to-parent talk that this is not right?

4. Give a presentation on the best episode of *Hidden Bloopers* that you have ever seen. Maybe your classroom teacher would let you re-create the best scenes from your favorite television program instead.

5. Sell a car, truck or van to your classmates. Have some car facts to back up your sales pitch.

6. Miss Honey is about to be replaced by the headmistress. She has asked you to speak on her behalf. How would you defend Miss Honey and prove that she is invaluable to the school and the children she teaches?

7. The school wants to put Matilda in a program for precocious children. Decide for yourself whether she would or wouldn't benefit from such a program. Then write your speech for or against including her in such a program.

8. The story ends with Matilda staying with Miss Honey. Give a talk on why she should stay with her parents.

9. Give a make-believe speech about the brightest child you ever met.

GA1459

HAND · HEAD · OUT · HAND · SPELL A VOCABULARY WORD

OUT

HEAD

From Handout to Head Out

Players move on the outside of the gameboard. They color in a box in the middle that combines with their outside

HEAD · OUT

HAND

HAND

STONE	LOCK	FIELD	ACHE
COME	WRIT-ING	DATED	SIDE
FIT	QUAR-TERS	SOME	BURST
BAG	STAND	LIGHT	BALL
RAIL	PUT	HOUSE	MADE

hand · out · head

HEAD

OUT

OUT

HAND

HEAD

word. First team to get three *out*, *head* and *hand* words or the first team to get four in a row wins (nine words in all).

HAND

HEAD

START · OUT · HEAD · HAND · OUT · LOSE A TURN

Basic construction and format for the game can be found on page 63. The object of the game will vary accordingly.

GA1459

Charlie and the Chocolate Factory

Horrible Surprises   Charlie's Challenge

Candy Bar Madness   Crazy Discoveries

Great Expectations   What a Contest!

Lead-Ins to Literature

This may be the start of every child's dream. Did you ever want to spend a day in a candy and toy factory? Imagine eating all the candy you could eat and playing with every device possible. Sound interesting, or would you rather stay home and count the spots on your refrigerator door? What was your answer to the question? Does the refrigerator door win again? In this story, people throughout the world will be fighting to find the winning passes to the world's greatest candy factory. Not all the winners were winners. Guess you'll have to read the story to find out when a winner is a loser. All right, let's get the show on the road.

1. What type of person would be the ideal head of the world's most famous candy factory? Would you expect the person to be young or old? Would it make any difference in the company's approach to selling candy? How? _____
   _____
   _____

2. Where do you think creative ideas for candy creations might come
   from in the story? _____
   _____
   _____

3. The candy factory assistants are strange creatures. What kind of workers do you think a creative author might put in such a factory? _____
   _____
   _____

4. Have you seen the Willy Wonka movie? If you have, how do you think the book might differ from the movie? What types of things could you put in a book that a movie director might find troublesome to include in a movie for children?_____
   _____
   _____

5. In what country would you place the world's greatest candy factory? Would you allow it to be visited by tourists? What would be the benefits of making it a tourist attraction? In addition to candy bars, would you sell other items like T-shirts and mugs to further spread the name of your company and its products? _____
   _____
   _____

6. If you worked for a candy firm, what job would you like to have? Explain. What salary would you expect?_____
   _____
   _____

7. You have been asked to include nasty children in a new story. What characteristics would these children have? _____
   _____
   _____

Just the Facts

Key points of Willy Wonka's story are listed in the subject category. First, design a statement on the importance of that subject to the story. Then write a factual question on the subject that a classmate can answer. Finally, make a five-part, factual mural using five key ideas from the story and five of your most scrumptious illustrations.

Subject: Gobstoppers

Statement: _____

Factual Question: _____

Subject: Oompa-Loompas

Statement: _____

Factual Question: _____

Subject: Grandpa Joe

Statement: _____

Factual Question: _____

Subject: Golden Tickets

Statement: _____

Factual Question: _____

Subject: Violet Beauregarde

Statement: _____

Factual Question: _____

Subject: The Salt Family

Statement: _____

Factual Question: _____

Subject: Prince Pondicherry

Statement: _____

Factual Question: _____

Subject: Mr. Bucket's Job

Statement: _____

Factual Question: _____

Create your mural on a sheet of art paper. Display this work sheet next to your mural.

GA1459

Just the Facts

1. Prince Pondicherry was from what country? _____

2. Where did Charlie's dad work? _____

3. What was loaded into the flying elevator at the end of the story? _____

4. What type of pillows and wallpaper were sold at Willy Wonka's famous factory?_____

5. Grandpa Joe said, "He is not," but what twelve words did the parents use to describe Willy Wonka? _____

   a. _____   g. _____

   b. _____   h. _____

   c. _____   i. _____

   d. _____   j. _____

   e. _____   k. _____

   f. _____   l. _____

6. How was Willy Wonka's boat described? _____

7. What were the names of the five children who won the golden ticket award for admission to the candy factory? Write one of his or her character traits next to each name.

   a. _____

   b. _____

   c. _____

   d. _____

   e. _____

8. How many years was Willy Wonka out of sight? _____

9. What was the name of the first candy bar that Charlie bought in his attempt at the gold ticket?_____

10. How much money was Charlie offered for his ticket?_____

11. Who was described as "a wart growing on your foot"?_____

12. What color were the factory's corridors?_____

13. Who reminded people of a rhinoceros? _____

14. How long did it take for the elevator to get a thousand feet in the sky?_____

15. What was made out of hot caramel? _____

16. Augustus had a hobby. What was it? _____

17. Mike Teavee was turned into millions of tiny_____

What Is Your Opinion?

1. Did the author make it believable that people all over the world could really go crazy over a visit to a candy factory? Explain the reasons for your answer.

2. Why do you think that children would want to read about other children being gobbled up and destroyed in a factory? Where is the humor in this happening to children?

3. No matter how nasty a child is, he or she should not be abused by some crazy factory president. What other things could Mr. Wonka have used to try to change the children's personalities?

4. What was the hardest thing to believe in the story? Why?

5. Do you think dreams are as important as people want you to think they are? What would a world without dreams be like? Are dreams necessary to insure a person's success?

6. What did you like best about the candy factory and the contest to be admitted to the factory?

7. How did you feel about the way the grandparents were portrayed in the story? In most books someone that lazy would not have been rewarded with the grand prize ticket.

8. What are the good and bad points of the contest? It certainly seemed like it helped to sell a lot of candy bars.

9. Do you think Mr. Wonka was a happy child? Why do you really think he devised the tour of his plant?

10. How many times do you think hopes can be dashed before someone gives up altogether? What do you think a person feels like when this happens? Can you understand the importance of overcoming disappointments? Explain your answer.

11. Who in the story do you think would make the best friend? The worst? Who aren't you sure about? Why?

GA1459

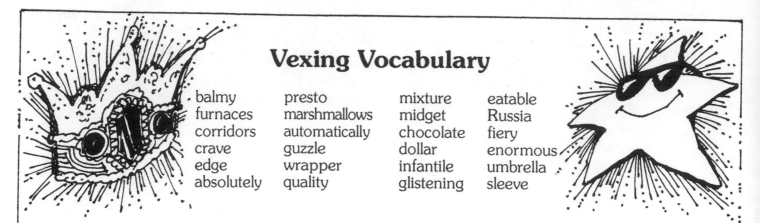

Vexing Vocabulary

balmy   presto   mixture   eatable
furnaces   marshmallows   midget   Russia
corridors   automatically   chocolate   fiery
crave   guzzle   dollar   enormous
edge   wrapper   infantile   umbrella
absolutely   quality   glistening   sleeve

Willy Wonka is inviting famous people to visit his chocolate factory. Your letter-writing skills will be challenged as you try to compose brief notes to each person below that will include as many of the vocabulary words as possible. Write a short note using five of the vocabulary words above. The note must reflect some part of each famous person's job or personality.

Kirby Puckett (baseball)
My factory is going to be an enormous hit with you. My chocolates will have you on the edge of your seat. You will absolutely forget about home runs after eating my candy. I _____
_____
_____

Whitney Houston (music)
_____
_____
_____

Roseanne Arnold (television)
_____
_____
_____

Bill Clinton (politics)
Roll up your sleeves, President Clinton, for the time of your life. _____
_____

Eddie Murphy (movies)
_____
_____
_____

Princess Diana (foreign affairs)
_____
_____
_____

Dracula (scary literature)
Hey! Big Guy! Visit my factory and you will crave chocolate instead of blood. No one ever _____
_____
_____

Pick three additional "short note characters" of your own and incorporate vocabulary words in their letters.

Compound Bird Words
Drills for Skills

Color me if you can find fifteen words . . . .

snow
shore
saw
cube
side
some
no

pa

light

look
night
sea
see

stand

to

How many compound words can you find hidden on this bird?

off
in
hold
house
foot

show
ice
one
body
on
time

1.
2.
3.
4.
5.

6.
7.
8.
9.
10.

11.
12.
13.
14.
15.

grand
out
up
boat
ball

Trace this bird three times. Hide three different activities, one on each bird. You might want to use synonyms, antonyms, homonyms, capitals or other ideas of your own.

One Letter at a Time Grid Activity
Short-Term Project

Game I

S	T	E	E	P
H	E	T	T	O
E	A	M	E	P
F	N	I	N	E
B	L	I	T	N

Examine the chart on the left. For every five-letter word you find, score 10 points; four-letter words score 8 points; three-letter words score 5 points; two-letter words score 2 points. Words can be only vertical or horizontal.

Game I

10 pointers	8 pointers	5 pointers	2 pointers
_____	_____	_____	_____
_____	_____	_____	_____
_____	_____	_____	_____
_____	_____	_____	_____
_____	_____	_____	_____

Game II

S	P	A	R	E
H	O	L	A	V
A	D	O	R	E
R	E	N	E	N
K	N	E	R	T

Game III

Draw a grid on the back of this paper. This now becomes a class activity. One letter at a time is given by various students and can be placed anywhere on an individual's grid. The 25th letter can be any one you need to complete your grid. Each person then adds up his or her score. High score wins.

Game II

10 pointers	8 pointers	5 pointers	2 pointers
_____	_____	_____	_____
_____	_____	_____	_____
_____	_____	_____	_____
_____	_____	_____	_____
_____	_____	_____	_____

GA1459

Candy Books
Ideas and Illustrations

You are about to become the author and illustrator of a book on candy for young children. Your task is to create an original way to introduce candy to young children, who make up a large portion of the buyers of candy. This task can be separated into two parts. The first part encourages you to complete the illustrations below of a candy hat, candy pillow, candy toothpaste, candy dog, candy shirt and candy bar. For the second part bring in candy bar wrappers in an original form.

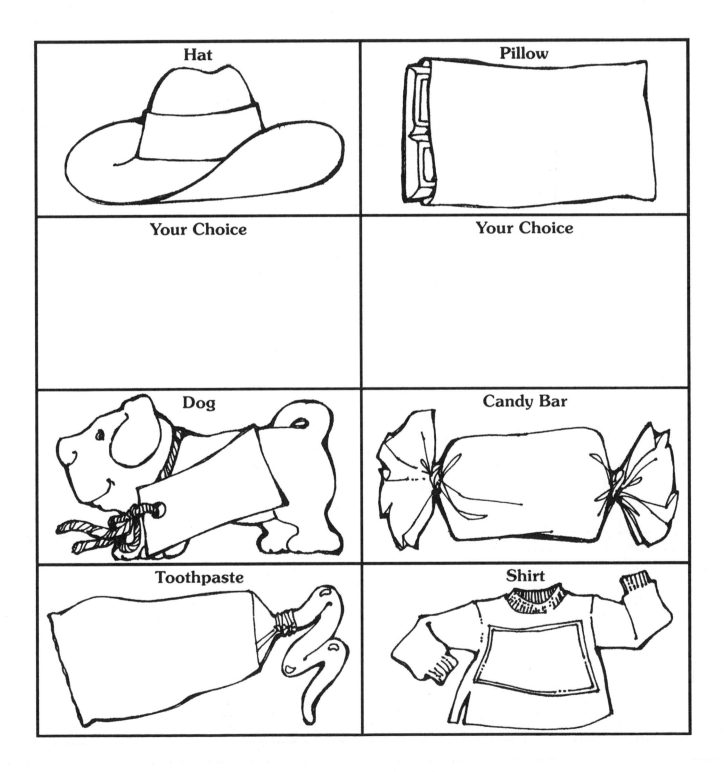

131

Student Research Suggestions

Advertising agencies handle a large number of different clients, from candy manufacturers to mall owners. Each agency employs a wide range of people from artists to salespeople. You are doing in-depth research on a local agency. Before doing so, you might want to do some research on the five top national agencies and the types of clients that they represent. Do these agencies concentrate on one area, or have you found that the more successful agencies are the ones that have clients in a variety of fields?

Interview

Your name: _____

Company being researched: _____

Reason for your selection: _____

Company's location: _____

Person interviewed: _____

Person's position in the company: _____

Years he or she has worked for this particular company: _____

Educational background: _____

Reason person selected this field: _____

Strong points brought to the job: _____

Five questions that you used for your interview:

1. _____
2. _____
3. _____
4. _____
5. _____

Types of clients the company represents: _____

_____

_____

After conducting your interview, use some of the ideas you learned to organize your own agency. Design your company's building and logo below. Surround your drawings with the features of your company. You might want to take the same questions above and answer them as if you were the president of the company who is being interviewed by a member of your class.

Teacher Suggestions

1. Discuss with your class how early kings and queens commissioned painters to paint for them. Then introduce some modern day workers who work for a commission before explaining that your class has been commissioned to design a mural for the side of a local building. Have your class design a painting for the side of a candy factory, public building, child care center or sports stadium.

2. After writing to the Hershey Corporation in Hershey, Pennsylvania, plan an imaginary class trip to the factory. Pack a lunch to eat in the classroom. Then have groups of children act like technicians in the many departments of the factory. They are to introduce the importance of their jobs and the products that they produce. They should also complete floor plans and diagrams of their departments. Mathematics can be incorporated by having each group hand in and explain its financial statement. Don't forget the importance of packaging and loading crews. Office workers should also be included in a group's presentation.

3. Have your class design a candy bar data base. Review the categories that may be included in the data base. They could include name, manufacturing company, nearest factory location, ingredients, packaging sizes (single bar, box, jumbo), other bars and candies produced by the company, other areas of manufacturing the company sponsors.

4. Introduce various diet plans that are now on the market, from Slim Fast™ to Weight Watchers™. Discusss their good and bad points. Impress on your class the seriousness of knowing what good food intake management is all about. Then, as a violation of everything you just taught them, have your students take a more humorous approach as they design the first candy diet.

5. Have your class design a candy bar top ten list with illustrations on one side of a giant piece of construction paper. On the other side have them design the most beneficial foods. Discuss "compare and contrast" writing techniques. Develop "compare and contrast" vocabulary words that should appear in a paper of a good writer.

6. Have your class create candy bar limericks: There was a young man from Pompeii/who ate candy bars most of the day/he knew it was wrong/to chew them so long/but he did it any weigh. (Get it? *Weigh*, not *way*.)

7. Create candy collages with your class. Each class member cuts out a candy bar wrapper and then has to hide it creatively in a picture. The scene represented in the picture may in no way represent the actual candy bar. A Milky Way™ candy bar may be incorporated in a picture of planets, asteroids and meteorites.

GA1459

Write Like a Master

Complete the five short story starters below with the theme that a candy bar or some kind of treat is involved in the problems presented. Your approach can be humorous, serious or out of this world, lip-smacking good.

Story Starter I

There goes a hand again. That is the fifth time this week someone almost selected me. Thank goodness my wrapper is ripped, or someone's teeth would surely take a chunk out of my chocolate coating. The only way I can stay out of someone's stomach is to _____

_____

_____

Story Starter II

Yes! Yes! The perfect candy bar! It will make children all over the world yell for more. Peanuts, caramel, yogurt, chocolate, and my mystery formula number forty-six. The formula was discovered by accident. I was _____

_____

_____

Story Starter III

Chocolate toothpaste looks like it is going to win the National Sweet Treat Award for the Outstanding Candy of the Year. The key to its success is its ability to _____

_____

_____

_____

Story Starter IV

This is a child's nightmare. I am allergic to candy. Every time I even think of candy I break out in ugly sores and blisters all over my body. So I happen to be exaggerating a little bit! It is true, though, I can't _____

_____

_____

_____

Story Starter V

Everywhere you look, you see ads for the new Candy Tree. They all ask, have you tried the Candy Tree? It comes in a small flowerpot and sells for ten dollars. It can actually grow candy in your room. The inventor says that _____

_____

_____

Public Speaking

Try organizing a one-minute talk on one of the following topics. Use the back of this paper to extend your thoughts on the particular topic that you choose. Collect three objects that have to do with your speech. After your speech explain how the three objects you selected relate to your speech. Place your opening thoughts on the lines below so your teacher can keep track of your speaking topic.

1. You are opening a candy factory in your hometown. Design the welcoming speech that you will give at the ribbon cutting ceremony. _____
_____

2. A teacher has asked you to talk to her class about the effects of sugar on your body. Do some sugar research before giving your speech. Try to include as many sugar facts as possible. _____
_____

3. You have designed a new candy with your favorite recording star on the wrapper. Introduce the candy bar to your classmates. Stress the involvement of your star. _____
_____

4. You are giving a news announcement for your local radio station. Try to somehow weave candy into your story. _____
_____

5. You are recommending two good books that would be excellent follow-ups after reading *Charlie and the Chocolate Factory*. Explain each book theme, reading level and the reasons it will make a good follow-up._____
_____

6. You have found one of the admission tickets to the Chocolate Factory. Explain your feelings to a group of your friends. Remember to include why you think this will be an exciting and rewarding experience. _____
_____

7. Introduce a new appliance to your classmates. Discuss the old uses for your appliance. Then introduce your ideas for modernization of the product. _____
_____

8. Robotics is being used in many industries throughout the United States. After reading three articles on robotics, present your ideas on how a robot might be used in your home, school or at a workplace. Be sure to introduce some ideas you learned about robotics in the articles that you have read. _____
_____

GA1459

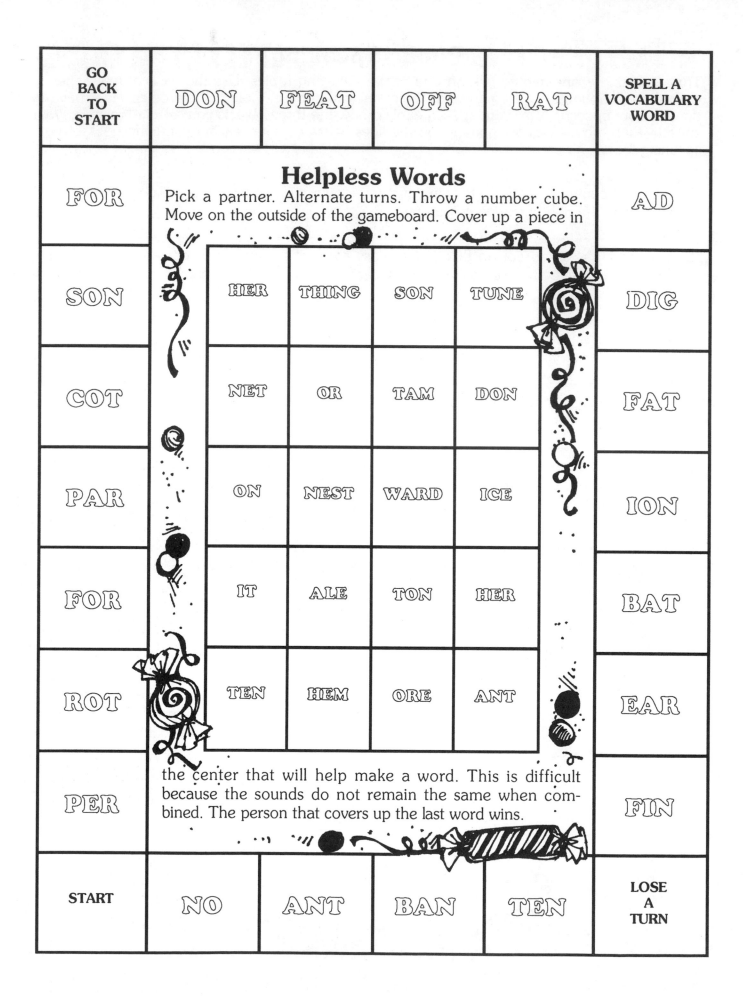

GO BACK TO START	DON	FEAT	OFF	RAT	SPELL A VOCABULARY WORD
FOR					AD
SON	HER	THING	SON	TUNE	DIG
COT	NET	OR	TAM	DON	FAT
PAR	ON	NEST	WARD	ICE	ION
FOR	IT	ALE	TON	HER	BAT
ROT	TEN	HEM	ORE	ANT	EAR
PER					FIN
START	NO	ANT	BAN	TEN	LOSE A TURN

Helpless Words

Pick a partner. Alternate turns. Throw a number cube. Move on the outside of the gameboard. Cover up a piece in the center that will help make a word. This is difficult because the sounds do not remain the same when combined. The person that covers up the last word wins.

136

GA1459

The Boy Who Could Talk with Animals

Hotel Guests

Turtle Soup

The Fishermen

Turtle Turnovers

Animal Communication

Coconut Disaster   Sea Adventure

GA1459

Lead-Ins to Literature

Have you ever been to a foreign country or to the islands surrounding the United States or Canada? The first thing that will happen to you is that someone will tell a story that is hard to believe. In *The Boy Who Could Talk with Animals*, you will find two unbelievable stories. A skull crushed by a falling coconut is the first of the two stories. The second is far stranger. It involves saving animals, a disappearance and many sightings of a child who seems to have the ability to communicate with animals. It is almost like a modern day *Tarzan*. See if you find the events in *The Boy Who Could Talk with Animals* on the believable side. Maybe the next time you visit the Bermuda Triangle, you will meet up with him.

1. Do you believe that it will one day be possible for humans to understand animals? How might this be accomplished? _____
_____
_____

2. Which animals do you think are the closest to humans in intelligence? What is the smartest animal that you have ever seen? Explain your choices. _____
_____
_____

3. Name three animals with whom you would like to communicate. Explain your reasons for choosing each animal. _____
_____
_____

4. The author picks a scenic island for staging his story. What other good locations could be selected for the theme of communicating with animals? _____
_____
_____

5. If you were taking a survey at a petting zoo for young children, what are the three top choices of animals that young children would like to ride? Do you think a large majority would pick your top choice, or do you think votes would be pretty evenly divided between your top choices? _____
_____
_____

6. What advice could you give a "city slicker" on the way to approach and handle marine life? __
_____
_____

7. Before reading the story, research two facts about the life span and intelligence of dolphins and turtles. _____
_____
_____

8. Would it be possible for someone to survive in the ocean if he or she was never allowed to touch land? How? _____
_____
_____

9. There are many ocean creatures on endangered species lists. Research two of them before starting the story. _____

10. Until this time, what is the most interesting animal story that you have read? _____
_____

GA1459

Just the Facts

Record the full sentence that contains the answer to each of these questions.

1. What was the composition of the plank that some idiotic man used to push the turtle?

   _____

2. What was Mr. Wasserman carrying when he was hit by the coconut? Please don't say "a lump on his head." _____

3. How old was David? _____

4. Five hundred and fifty represents what in the story? _____

5. What two reasons for the missing boy were given by the hotel manager? _____

6. Three uses for the turtle were cheered by the people on the beach. What were they? _____

   _____

7. "Dead as a _____" was the phrase used by the maid as she explained Mr. Wasserman's condition.

8. What did the green lizards do after the courting dance? _____

9. How were the Bermuda shorts described that were mentioned in the story? _____

10. What word was used to describe the size of the turtle, and what two meanings can you give for this word? _____

11. Write questions that will have these words as their answers.

    a. the yacht _____

    b. Jamaica _____

    c. Coral Reefs _____

    d. binoculars _____

    e. lethal _____

    f. three times as fast _____

    g. due north _____

    h. sunburned _____

    i. hooded black eyes _____

What Is Your Opinion?

1. If you were the illustrator of this story, what ideas would you include in the cover of the book to attract people to the story? Do you think having people on the beach with sticks raised over a turtle would be a good approach?

   _____

   _____

2. What is your opinion about hunting turtles for their shells or using them to make soup or turtle steaks? If this were the only way an island native could survive, would you change your point of view?

   _____

   _____

3. If you were David, would you have left your family for this turtle? Did David have any other choices he could have made?

   _____

   _____

4. Turtles are one of the animals that live the longest. Some live for as long as two hundred years. What contributes to their long life?

   _____

   _____

5. Explain why people in a crowd would act differently than they would if they were on their own.

   _____

   _____

6. What animal could we learn the most from if we really studied it? Explain your selection.

   _____

   _____

7. What places in the book would you like to visit? Are you the type of person who would enjoy an island vacation or a vacation in the mountains? Big city? Jungle?

   _____

   _____

8. If members of your family were missing on an island vacation, what would you do that David's parents didn't do?

   _____

   _____

9. Would you like to have a friend like David? What would his strong and weak points be?

   _____

   _____

10. Would you consider riding a sea turtle into the lagoon of an island?

    _____

    _____

11. Did you think at any point in the story that David would have returned to the hotel and to his family?

    _____

    _____

12. What was the author trying to say in writing this story? Did the story have any special message for children/adults?

    _____

    _____

GA1459

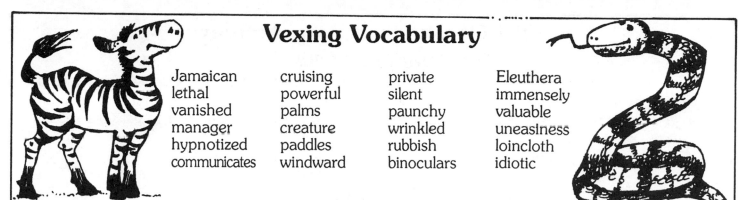

Vexing Vocabulary

Jamaican	cruising	private	Eleuthera
lethal	powerful	silent	immensely
vanished	palms	paunchy	valuable
manager	creature	wrinkled	uneasiness
hypnotized	paddles	rubbish	loincloth
communicates	windward	binoculars	idiotic

A "fractional" vocabulary word is a word that has a smaller word of three or more letters in it. One and two-letter words within a larger word are not accepted for this activity. Three blanks are provided for you. Place the original word in blank one. In blank two, place the smaller word contained in the original. Some originals have more than one word hidden in them. Try to select the smaller word with the most letters. In blank three you will form a fraction by placing the number of letters in the smaller word over the number of letters in the original. Try to remember the smaller words in the original when it comes to spelling test time. This activity is designed to help make you a better speller.

	Original	Hidden Word	Fraction
1.	lethal	let	$^3/_6 = {}^1/_2$
2.			
3.			
4.			
5.			
6.			
7.			
8.			
9.			
10.			
11.			
12.			
13.			

Try doing this with the names of animals you know. Add your suggestions to the six animals already given below.

python	bear	zebra	fox	hippopotamus	shark

GA1459

Oh! O! What a Crazy Activity
Drills for Skills

Your vocabulary sense will be challenged with this "o" activity. The first clue will give you an everyday word. The second clue repeats the first answer. Only this time the letter *o* is added to the end of the word generated by the first clue. Add an *o* to every first answer to get your second answer.

Example: to come together   dessert treat
        jell   Jell-O™

1. a color _____   change again _____
2. two cups_____   a horse with spots_____
3. prison room_____   musical instrument _____
4. two-sport athlete Jackson _____   ghost sound _____
5. in the direction of _____   also _____
6. orange breakfast drink _____   type of dance_____
7. mineral-bearing rock_____   type of cookie _____
8. type of cherry _____   five in a row game _____
9. wedding band _____   one of the Beatles_____
10. young girl_____   used to rope a horse_____
11. body bladder _____   famous wine family_____
12. Spanish cheer _____   butter substitute_____
13. rough edge of plant or material _____   pack-carrying donkey_____

Write clues for these words: *concert, came, disc.* Then try to complete a similar activity by finding ten words to which the letter *a* can be added to make a new word (*are/area, bet/beta, Meg/mega, tamp/Tampa, Ann/Anna*).

The Coconut Shop
Ideas and Illustrations

You are the owner of the most famous coconut shop in the world. People marvel at the unlimited number of uses of the coconut that you keep developing. Not only have you come up with hundreds of juices, lotions and creams made from the inside of the coconut, but you have devised many uses for the coconut shell. You have been asked to display your six favorite coconut designs at a local museum. Fill out the form below and then place your most original designs on the items below.

What is your name at school? _____

In your shop who are you known as? _____

What is the name of your shop? _____

Where is it located? _____

_____

What are the three most common coconut products that you sell? _____

_____

What creations would you consider your most original ones? _____

_____

_____

Enlarge your best coconut product on the back of this page.

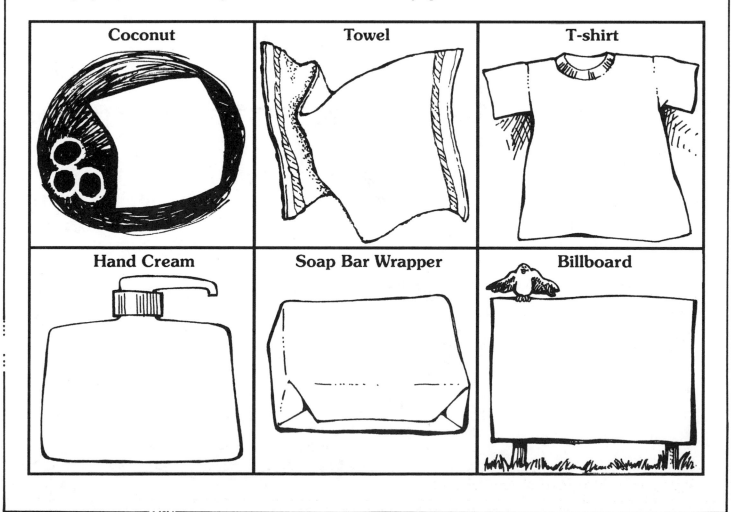

| Coconut | Towel | T-shirt |
| Hand Cream | Soap Bar Wrapper | Billboard |

GA1459

Alphabetical Time
Short-Term Project

These clocks can be used to discover new words. When a time is given to you, look first at the letter the hour hand would be pointing to. Record that letter. Follow that letter with the letter(s) in the middle of the clock face. Follow these letters with the letter the minute hand would be pointing to. How many times will the clocks below give you a vocabulary word? Solve the times with words below; then see if you can find ten additional times for each clock that spell words on the following page.

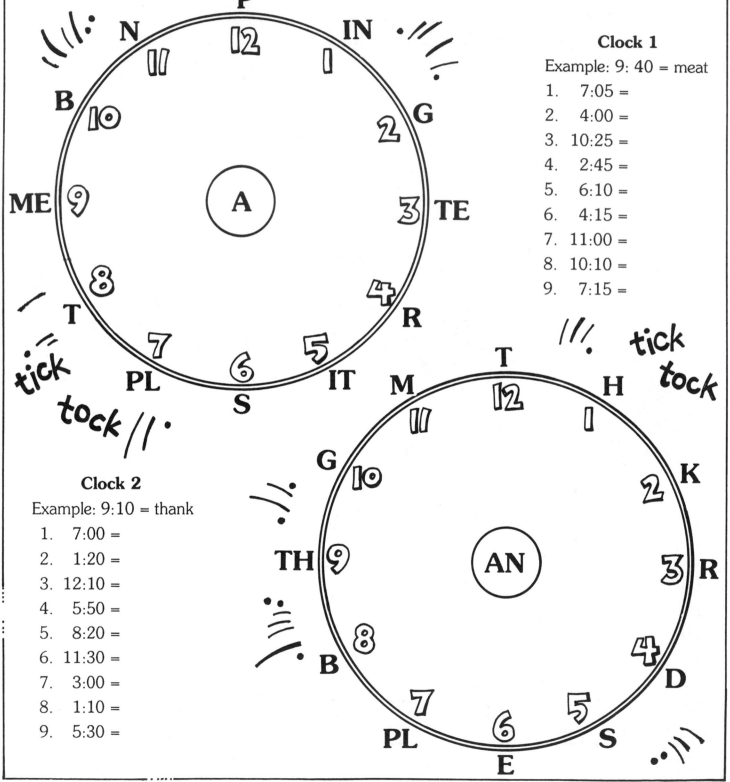

Clock 1

Example: 9: 40 = meat

1. 7:05 =
2. 4:00 =
3. 10:25 =
4. 2:45 =
5. 6:10 =
6. 4:15 =
7. 11:00 =
8. 10:10 =
9. 7:15 =

Clock 2

Example: 9:10 = thank

1. 7:00 =
2. 1:20 =
3. 12:10 =
4. 5:50 =
5. 8:20 =
6. 11:30 =
7. 3:00 =
8. 1:10 =
9. 5:30 =

GA1459

Alphabetical Time
Short-Term Project
Blank Student Work Sheet

This clock can be used to discover new words. When a time is given to you, look first at the letter the hour hand is facing. Record that letter. Follow that letter with the one or two letters in the middle of the clock face. Follow these letters with the letter the minute hand is facing. Design your own work sheet after filling in the letters on the clock below. Review the previous page before making your selections. On the left, write ten times that will give words that your classmates could solve. On the right side of the work sheet, give your classmates words that they will turn into times.

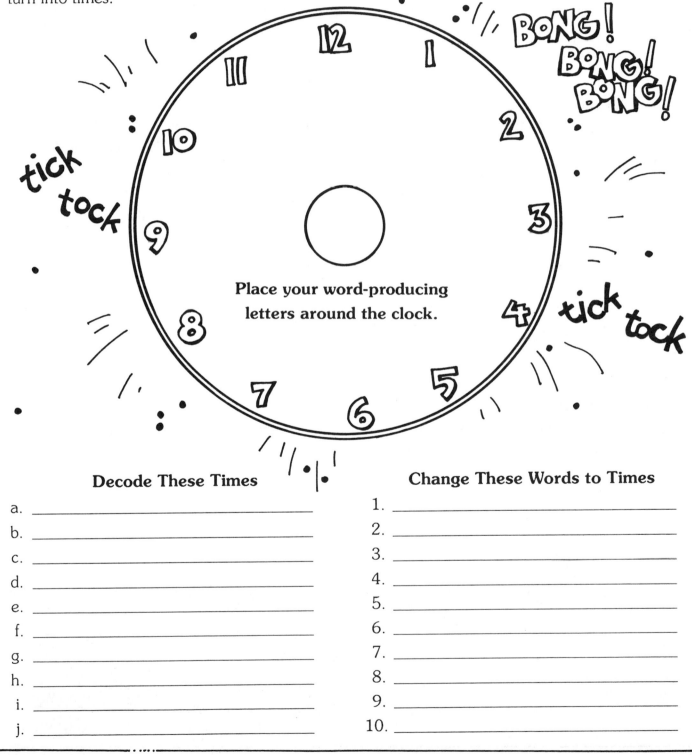

Place your word-producing letters around the clock.

Decode These Times	Change These Words to Times
a. _____	1. _____
b. _____	2. _____
c. _____	3. _____
d. _____	4. _____
e. _____	5. _____
f. _____	6. _____
g. _____	7. _____
h. _____	8. _____
i. _____	9. _____
j. _____	10. _____

GA1459

Write Like a Master

Complete the five short story starters below that center on the theme of an animal that is in some way involved with solving the problems presented. Your approach can be humorous or serious.

Story Starter I

It happened again. Brutus put his paw on the correct answer in my math book. It was almost like he was listening to my thoughts. I was thinking to myself that there was no way I could solve that problem. All of a sudden, wham, a paw landed on the correct answer. I thought of the next hard problem, and yes, you know the answer. Brutus solved it again. Yesterday he helped me with my spelling by _____

_____

_____

_____

Story Starter II

There has to be something in this file that will give us a clue to what happened. It looks like the animals housed in this cage were able to learn anything that was taught to them. There is evidence that they_____

_____

_____

_____

Story Starter III

Boomerang and I have won the National Frisbee™ Championship four years in a row. Our most famous trick is now copied by every team that we compete against. It starts by _____

_____

_____

_____

Story Starter IV

This toucan can repeat anything you say to him. The only problem is that he says everything backwards. Have you ever heard the national anthem sung backward? What is even funnier is his ability to _____

_____

_____

_____

Story Starter V

My cat is in the new *Guinness Book of World Records*. She almost made it last year for tightrope walking. This year's feat was far superior. She is the only cat who _____

_____

_____

_____

GA1459

Student Research Suggestions

1. Imagine you are in charge of the turtle habitat exhibit at your local zoo. Research the outlets in your area that are capable of providing you with information about the care and breeding of turtles in captivity.

2. Create four new characters for the Teenage Mutant Ninja Turtles. Try to name them after four scientists, sports figures or historical characters. Design each new member of the group so it inherits two characteristics from the original character for whom it was named.

3. The "carapace" is the turtle's upper shell. The "plastron" is the turtle's stomach protection. Design a mini illustrated chart showing other animals that might be considered members of the body armor family.

4. Bog turtles are a few inches long. The leatherback turtle is close to nine feet long. Research these two turtles, and then find another species that differs that much in size. What kind of comparisons can you make about these two species?

5. The leatherback has no shell. Its tough outer skin is what protects it. Make a top ten chart. Rank the ten animals that have the strongest body protection. Where did you place the turtle in this ranking system?

6. A gopher tortoise can dig a hole ten feet deep to protect itself from the heat and its enemies. What characteristics does it have that compare to other burrowing animals like the fox, rabbit, prairie dog or mole?

7. Create a turtle "believe it or not." Instead of naming it after Mr. Ripley, use your own name.
   a. Even though some turtles live to be over one hundred years old, they reach their maximum size at the end of the first ten years.
   b. Sea turtles can lay two hundred eggs.
   c. Musk turtles hiss like snakes when in a fight.
   d. The Indian word *terrapin* means "turtle."

8. Some turtles hibernate while others can be found moving around the bottoms of frozen lakes in the winter. Research information about hibernating animals for a mini mural.

9. Your fishing boat has a turtle flag on the flagpole. It is the flag of a group known as the Screaming Turtles. Design this organization, concentrating on its goals and ways it is educating school children to better understand the ocean and the ocean's inhabitants.

10. Make a "largest of the species" illustrated chart. Pick ten animal classifications and list the size of the largest in that particular species. Turtles: The giant tortoise of the Galapagos Islands weighs over five hundred pounds.

GA1459

Teacher Suggestions

1. Have your class research the migration habits of three different sea creatures. Try to pick three creatures that aren't the most well-known in your classroom. Have the class pay particular attention to the significance of the distance traveled, time taken, reason for the movement (birth of young, after food, change in water temperature) and change in the animal or its family upon its return.

2. Compare the cost of having as pets two animals that are in the same family but of different sizes. Have each member of your class make a mini chart comparing the cost of keeping a little turtle in a bowl to keeping a giant sea turtle; a kitten to a female lion; a canary to a California condor. Encourage research in the eating habits of each creature, possible size of adult, cost of building a suitable habitat, local licenses and length of life.

3. Write to a local high school, college or university alumni association to convince them to change their school mascot to a turtle. Have your students organize and present their findings as to why the turtle would make an excellent symbol for any group. Can you picture Pennsylvania State University's football team being called the Nittany Turtles instead of the Nittany Lions?

4. Have your class design an animal collage using the outline of a turtle's body to house each of the pictures your students have collected of their particular animal.

5. Have your class create acronyms, bumper stickers and T-shirts for a group of animal rights activists who study and protect the giant sea turtle. (Examples: I brake for sea turtles. It is nine o'clock. Do you know where your turtle is? Today I saved a turtle. Make a turtle your friend, not your soup. TFT [Turtles For Tots]. Have you called your turtle today?)

6. Create a tourist attraction with your class called Turtle World. Design five jobs for which the students in your class might apply. Have each child design a ride or a viewing area that might interest young children. What turtles would be featured in your natural habitat?

7. Invite a fish store owner to class to discuss the business, tank types and design, costs and the job opportunities creative people who are fascinated by sea life might want to pursue.

8. Have half the class write "Mom/Dad, I am going to get on this turtle's back and ride away," while the other half of the class writes "Son/Daughter, there is no way you're going to go anywhere on a turtle or any other animal, at least not until you have cleaned your room."

9. Have your class research "the ideal place for a vacation." Have them write letters to each location to see if turtles are allowed to be kept in the room.

GA1459

Public Speaking

Public speaking practice isn't designed so you can just give a formal speech to a group of people. It is designed so you can get the maximum from your mind anytime you are in a "speaking position." If David could have presented his thoughts in a clear manner to the crowd, maybe he could have saved the turtle. You're responsible for a one-minute speech on any one of the topics listed below. (There is room for you to enter topics of your own at the bottom of the page. Please check with your teacher for approval.) There is a space after each topic for brief notes. This will give your teacher an opportunity to see that you're headed in the right direction before actually giving your speech.

1. You are explaining to a fishing group the benefits of fish farming. That is replacing the fish that are caught with fish from nurseries and spawning plants. You are a conservationist but also an environmentalist. Include a discussion about water pollution in your speech.

   _____

   _____

2. You are giving a speech about saving the giant sea turtle. Include some facts about its eating and breeding habits.

   _____

   _____

3. You are speaking to a group of shell collectors. You are recommending a trip to Sanibel Island in Florida. Highlight some of the unusual shells and formations an avid collector might find there.

   _____

   _____

4. David is your eight-year-old brother. He has told you about wanting to ride this giant turtle and living away from his family. Would you encourage this in a talk with him, or would you convince him to stay home and search for other methods that would mesh with his ability to communicate with animals? Write your heart-to-heart talk below.

   _____

   _____

5. You are giving a speech to raise money for a turtle refuge. How would you convince your audience to financially support this cause?

   _____

   _____

Place three of your own speech topics integrating sea animals below.

GO BACK TO START	DIS	RE	UN	IM	SPELL A VOCABULARY WORD

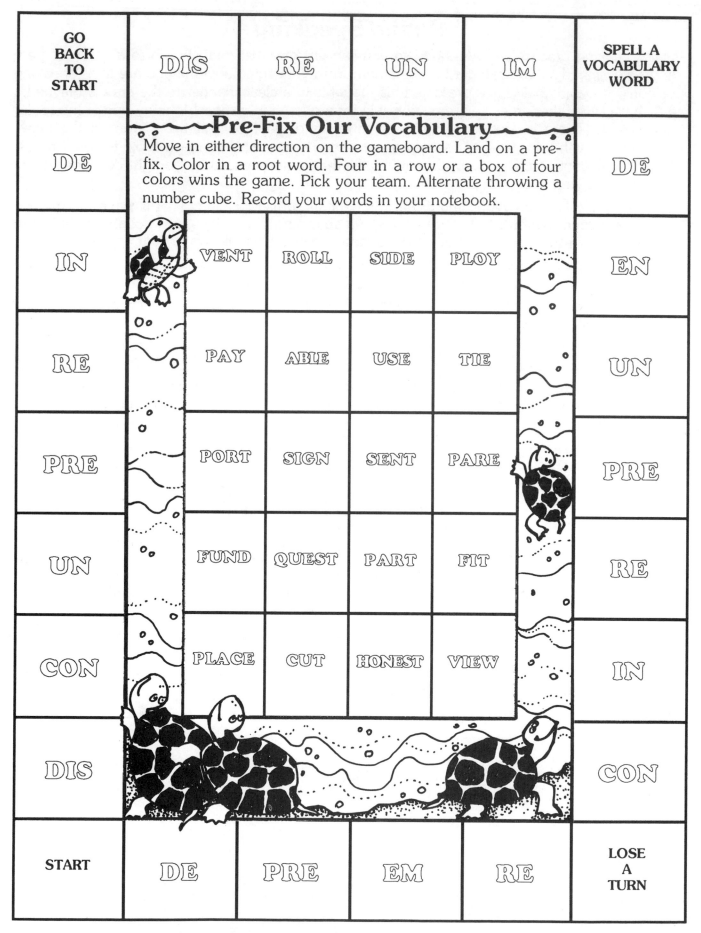

Pre-Fix Our Vocabulary

Move in either direction on the gameboard. Land on a prefix. Color in a root word. Four in a row or a box of four colors wins the game. Pick your team. Alternate throwing a number cube. Record your words in your notebook.

DE	VENT	ROLL	SIDE	PLOY	DE
IN	PAY	ABLE	USE	TIE	EN
RE	PORT	SIGN	SENT	PARE	UN
PRE	FUND	QUEST	PART	FIT	PRE
UN	PLACE	CUT	HONEST	VIEW	RE
CON					IN
DIS					CON
START	DE	PRE	EM	RE	LOSE A TURN

Basic construction and format for the game can be found on page 63. The object of the game will vary accordingly.

Write Like a Master
Additional Suggestions

Teacher Note:

As soon as my classes "hit" the room, there are three to five Write Like a Master themes on the board. This gives each student a chance to calm down and for me to take roll, settle disputes, collect money and talk with parents. It is also a message to students that as soon as they arrive, there is work to do. I remind students that each day there will be choices of different writing situations. Very rarely will they be themselves, though experience in a certain topic will add to their compositions. I try to explain each theme and offer suggestions on the directions that they might take if they choose to write in that particular area. We are lucky to have a computer laboratory next door to our room. Anytime the lab isn't being used, we can take our stories, enhance them with pictures and make easy-to-read printouts for student portfolios, class bulletin boards or a school newspaper.

Here are fifty additional follow-ups to the "Write Like a Master" sections in each of the Roald Dahl stories that you have just completed. They should give you a wealth of additional creative writing formats. The wide variety of writing experiences will broaden and sharpen your writing skills. You may continue the starters below or spin off in directions of your own. Space is limited on these blanks, so use the back of the paper to extend your ideas. Have a friend illustrate each of your selections, then make a fancy writing portfolio for your work.

1. My nickname is going to be "Oops." Every time I wear something nice–Oops!–food, ice cream or chocolate lands in my lap. Last night was the classic "oops." I _____
   _____
   _____

2. Welcome to Seat Belt Safety class. Each of you is here for not wearing your seat belt. The accidents you were in might not have been preventable, but you would be free of injury if you had worn your seat belts. It doesn't take a genius to _____
   _____
   _____

3. Last night my brother changed into Batman right in front of my eyes. His friend Billy drove up on our lawn in the Batmobile to pick him up. Billy doesn't drive! They _____
   _____
   _____

4. What do you like best about going to the movies? To me it is seeing everything on a giant screen rather than a little television at home. I also like _____
   _____
   _____

GA1459

5. Last night this finger was slammed in a door. You'll notice how it is swollen and discolored. The stitches _____

_____

_____

6. The baby is very sick. The famine has lasted for over three months. You can see the bones on her arms, and her stomach is bloated from the lack of food. I don't_____

_____

_____

7. The Aqualab is a self-supporting community at the bottom of the Pacific Ocean. We will not see the surface of the earth for two years. Each of us was chosen for a reason. My name is _____. I am the only _____-year-old in the community. I was chosen _____

_____

_____

8. The Mathelmut is something that no school child should be without. It sells for $99 and has four modes that will amaze you. In the first mode it can answer any math problem that you have in your mind. The second mode allows you to _____

_____

_____

9. Where is Sarah the Problem Solver? Every time I get into a jam she seems to have the solution for getting me out of it. This one is a real tough one. It seems that _____

_____

_____

10. You must be an earthling. Everyone on Stemra has two heads! The advantages are endless. My three favorites are _____

_____

_____

11. Both of my feet are stuck in the tar. If I slip out of my shoes and leave them here, Mom will kill me. My sister thinks we might be able to lasso my shoes later. I think _____

_____

_____

12. The Brockton water slide is the longest slide in the world. It winds through almost two miles of mazes, strange chutes and weird falls. The two most difficult sections_____

_____

_____

13. People in Heightsville are among the strangest in the world. When they are born, they are as tall as they're going to get. For each year that they live, they get smaller. This has caused a lot of problems over the years. It also has its good points too. You see, you _____

_____

_____

GA1459

14. My back hurts from sitting at this computer for so long. Computers should come with massage chairs. That way, when you are working or sitting for long periods of time, you can just push one of three buttons and instantly you _____

_____

_____

15. Our rain falls in three different flavors. If it rains in the morning, it tastes like milk. In the afternoon it has a soda flavor. Last night's rain had a new taste. It_____

_____

_____

16. I always sit by the window. It is great for daydreaming, seeing the first snow or being warmed a little extra by the sun. After last week, though, someone else can have the window seat. I was playing with a rubber band and_____

_____

_____

17. Football is a dangerous sport. Two of my friends _____

_____

_____

18. My real name is Gopher Pierce. You are already laughing. I can tell! It wasn't my fault that my parents_____

_____

_____

19. Yuck, this apple has a worm in it! Half of the worm is missing! Oh! Do you think that I ____

_____

_____

20. The fog is so thick that you can write your name in it. The strange animal cries seem to be coming from my left. Now some cries are to my right. It, or they, seem to be surrounding me. There was no need for me to be investigating the strange sightings of local hunters this late at night. I am the only one that believed that _____

_____

_____

21. The Come-Together Ball is our newest creation and one of the best-sellers from my Toytronics Manufacturing Company. When you throw the ball off a wall or a hard surface, it seems to break into different pieces. Just press the "back together" button on our hand-held "beamer" and the pieces reform into the original ball. Some of the pieces can be as far as three inches away from the ball's core. Mini computer chips on each piece are the secret that pulls the pieces together. How the pieces pull together to form the exact starting shape is something that I can't share with you. Secrets are secrets! However, I will tell you about our latest project, even though it is not patented yet. It is called a Timeittron. It is _____

_____

_____

22. The scientific consequences are endless. It won't stick to anything, and it is impossible to hold in your hand. I combined _____

_____

Three immediate uses for this mercury-like plastic are _____

_____

23. Sitting here on the beach watching the sunset reminds me of _____

_____

_____

24. Did you see the size of Columbus's ship? This classroom is bigger than the whole top deck. His sleeping quarters were the size of our walk-in coatroom. How in the world did thirty men cross the Atlantic in that ship? If I were on the first voyage to the New World, I probably _____

_____

_____

25. No way am I going to kiss that sleeping woman and break the witch's spell! First, I don't believe in witches, and second, I don't believe in magic spells. You actually believe that story about biting into an apple? How could _____

_____

_____

26. Rub this mud all over your arms and face, and it will _____

_____

_____

27. Hello, Mr. President. If you have a minute, I have a couple of ideas that might solve some of our country's most pressing problems. Take, for instance, the problem with _____

_____

_____

28. She walked right through the wall. I've seen the Road Runner do it while running from the Coyote but never a living, breathing human being. I thought she used mirrors or trick photography. When I reached the spot she passed through, I found it to be solid brick. The wall seemed to be hot. Stuck in the wall was a piece of material from her cape. I pulled, but it wouldn't come out. No one _____

_____

_____

29. Please hold my hand while crossing the street. There is just too much traffic. The drivers just go _____

_____

_____

30. Did you ever play catch in total darkness? There is a new ball called the Glow Ball that allows you to do just that. You break this stick and insert it in the ball. The liquid in the stick glows for an hour. The sticks come in a five-pack. When you throw the ball to a partner, it is like catching a shooting star. Last night _____

_____

31. Echo Mountain should be the eighth Wonder of the World. It is awe inspiring. We go there to _____

_____.

_____

32. Did you ever take a ride on a camel? It is a cross between riding a roller coaster and riding a

_____

_____

_____

33. We've been stuck in this elevator for four hours. The last place you want to be during an earthquake is in an elevator. Yet, who knew an earthquake was going to hit? The air is starting to get thin. I am wondering if anyone even knows we are here. What if everything around here is destroyed? We may never be rescued. I can't think of _____

_____

_____

34. I am in the middle of an escalator that is going upward, but I'm not moving. People are passing right by me, but it is as if I am standing still. People have brushed past me and talked to me, but I am not moving. I tried _____

_____

_____

35. The kayak races are ready to begin. Last year's race _____

_____

_____

36. The people of the planet Plethar are the most honest, likable and caring people in our galaxy. They have to be. There is a chemical in their brain stems that causes a part of their bodies to dissolve if they steal, try to hurt someone or are mean. There is another planet in our galaxy where a similar thing happens. All the children _____

_____

_____

37. The Penguin is the newest dance craze sweeping the country and our school. Paula Abdul and Michael Jackson performed the dance at the MTV Music Awards. Now everyone_____

_____

_____

38. The elm tree is one of the most beautiful shade trees native to the United States. The owl sitting in my elm tree is just the opposite. He starts "who"ing at 10 p.m. and _____

_____

_____

39. Rollerblades are better than normal four-wheel roller skates. You can make faster stops, shorter turns and be far more creative in your skating moves. The Skatedrome is_____

_____

_____

GA1459

40. If you research the story of the Greek philosopher Diogenes, you will find that he lived in a tub. Today 100,000 homeless Americans don't even have a tub that they can live in. The homeless should be one of the three major issues in this year's local and national elections.

_____

_____

_____

41. I wish I could speak more than one language. When you speak more than one language, it seems more of the world is open to you. You can relate to people better and you have an understanding of how _____

_____

_____

42. Today is an ideal day to sell my younger brother and sister. If no one will buy them, perhaps someone will trade an old bike, baseball glove or dance shoes for them. Mom will be pleased if I split the money with her. Dad will _____

_____

_____

43. Jumping off a bridge with a rubber band-like rope tied to my legs doesn't sound like Sunday excitement to me. My brain is scrambled enough! If the rope breaks, my head will be like a cracked egg yoke. Why would anyone _____

_____

_____

44. For once in your life, please just leave it alone! I _____

_____

_____

45. I like being read to before I go to bed each night. It is a special time. Mom is the best reader, but Gramps is by far the best storyteller. Last night he had me hanging on his every word as he told the story of old Grimsley. It all started ten years ago in Billow Hospital._____

_____

_____

46. You can pick at this cotton candy cone forever! It just keeps on replacing itself. It changes flavors and doesn't seem at all sticky. The cotton candy booth was set up right next to the fortune-teller. Sounds like the movie *Big*. Only in this case, things can't be returned to normal. There is no way that you can stop this cone from _____

_____

_____

47. I fell asleep at the movies. Dad had to carry me _____

_____

_____

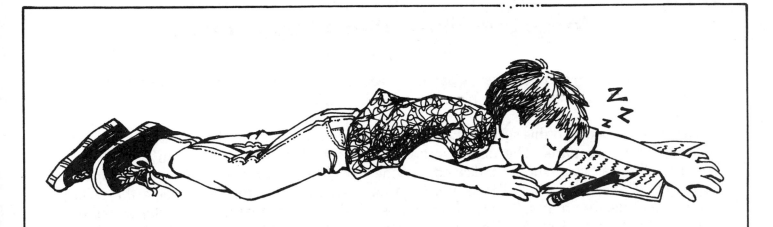

48. What a brave five-year-old Susan is! My poor sister's thumb has been stuck in the bathtub drain all day. The fire department, police department and plumber still haven't been able to get it out. Next, they are going to _____

_____

_____

49. You won't believe what I found growing in my hair last night! It was enough to _____

_____

_____

50. This is the last Master Write that I will ever write. Tomorrow I am going on a creative writing strike. I am sure I can get my classmates to join me. That is, everyone except Jamaal and Deidra. They both love writing and reading. I wonder what causes someone to love writing and reading? It probably is contagious or maybe the _____

_____

_____

Ideas and Illustrations Supplement
Bulletin Boards

Dear cartographers, architects, sign painters, teachers, students, and bulletin board makers of America, . . . If you are a doodler, please join in this activity.

There are nine pages in this section. Each page represents a month of the school year. The page is divided into two parts. The upper section contains an idea for a classroom or hall bulletin board for the particular month indicated. Teachers might want to take a piece of transparency paper, trace the bulletin board idea, put it on an overhead projector, and outline the enlarged image the projector creates. The lower section is a bulletin board that has been started but needs student help to complete. Students are asked to give their input as to the direction additional writing and illustration should take. Please complete the student bulletin board with your original and humorous ideas. A monthly clothesline of student bulletin boards makes a great display. A blank bulletin board has been provided below for students who would like to create a bulletin board from scratch. Students can use this blank board to create ideas for their other subjects as well. Transfer your best ideas to 11" x 14" (27.94 x 35.56 cm) art paper and pin the best work of the class up in the hallway. Try having a bulletin board contest after your teacher gives you a general theme for your original work.

Student name _____

My bulletin board theme is _____

Add your own ideas to each of the bulletin boards below.

Bulletin Board Idea for September
September Will Nourish Your Body

Student-Developed Bulletin Board for September
"Fall" into These Good Habits

Write a good habit on each parachute. Design the jumper's outfit and each parachute.

GA1459

Add your own ideas to each of the bulletin boards below.

Bulletin Board Idea for October
Even Vampires Work on Their Vocabulary

Student-Developed Bulletin Board for October
Pumpkin Patch Patter

What messages for October can you think of to put on the six pumpkins above?

GA1459

Add your own ideas to each of the bulletin boards below.

Bulletin Board Idea for November
Look at the Progress of These Pilgrims

Look at the Progress of These Pilgrims

Student-Developed Bulletin Board for November
November Needs

November Needs

pumpkin

pecan pie

pants

jacket

turkey

warm clothing

Add your additional needs to this November bulletin board.

Add your own ideas to each of the bulletin boards below.

Bulletin Board Idea for December
Dialing December

Student-Developed Bulletin Board for December
December's Dreams

Draw a dream scene above each head.

GA1459

Add your own ideas to each of the bulletin boards below.

Bulletin Board Idea for January
Take a January Journey Through a New Book

Student-Developed Bulletin Board for December
Make January a Jubilee of Learning

Create a book, faraway land, a store, a gameboard and an idea of your own for a January Jubilee.

Add your own ideas to each of the bulletin boards below.

Bulletin Board Idea for February
The V's for February Study

Student-Developed Bulletin Board for February
Cures for an Achy Breaky Heart

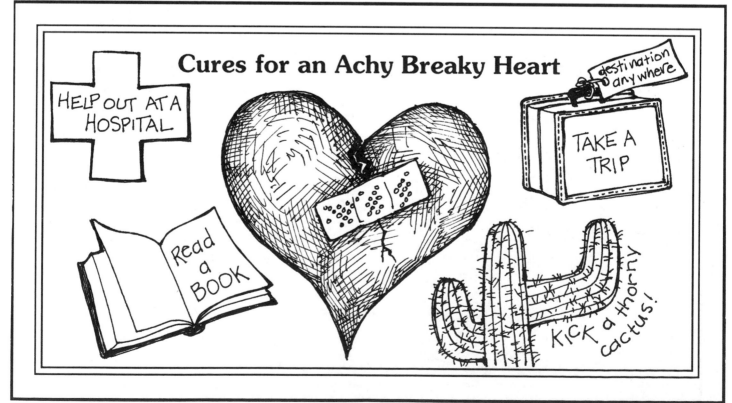

Can you think of three things to do to repair a broken heart? Design three humorous ones also.

Add your own ideas to each of the bulletin boards below.

Bulletin Board Idea for March
Causes to March Up and Be Counted

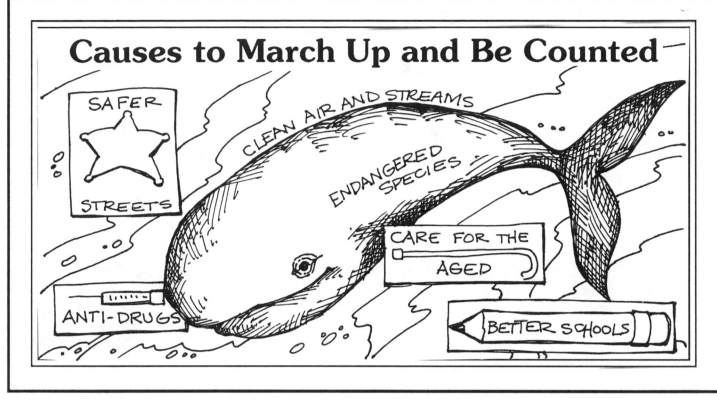

Student-Developed Bulletin Board for March
"March" into the World of Science

What other areas of science would you encourage students to march into for further study?

GA1459

Add your own ideas to each of the bulletin boards below.

Bulletin Board Idea for April
The Splashes of Spring

The Splashes of Spring

Longer Days

Nature Awakes

Brighter Colors in Clothing

School Experiments

Walks in Warmer Sunshine

Baseball Begins

Student-Developed Bulletin Board for April
Fill Your Mind at the Education Spring

Fill Your Mind at   the Education Spring

Art

Math

Science

Social Studies

Literature

With what new ideas would you like to fill up your mind?

GA1459

Add your own ideas to each of the bulletin boards below.

Bulletin Board Idea for May
"May" Your Books Be as Great as These Roald Dahl Classics

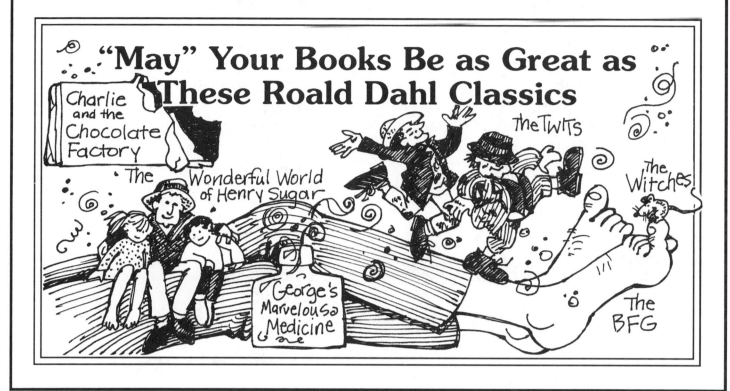

Student-Developed Bulletin Board for May
May Your Giant Peach Be as Interesting as James's Peach Was

What unique things would you put on a peach? On your own, try to create two bulletin boards for June, July and August.

GA1459

Answer Key

Just the Facts, page 3
1. big friendly giant
2. dormitory
3. the witching hour
4. the last page
5. snoozcumbers
6. blew dreams
7. Answers will vary.
8. *Nicholas Nickleby*
9. north
10. white as a sheet
11. coughed
12. blue
13. trogglehumper, bogthumper, grob-switcher
14. King of Sweden, Sultan of Baghdad

Drills for Skills, page 6
1. stump $1/5$
2. umpire $3/6 = 1/2$
3. clump $1/5$
4. trumpet $2/7$
5. dump $1/4$
6. grumpy $1/6$
7. hump $1/4$
8. mumps $1/5$
9. chum $1/4$
10. Humphrey $2/8 = 1/4$
11. jumping $2/7$
12. pump $1/4$
13. rumble $2/6 = 1/3$
14. Rumpelstiltskin $4/15$
15. plump $1/5$

Drills for Skills, page 23
2. oxen
3. oxymoron
4. chicken pox
5. Chicago White Sox
6. toxic
7. Oxford
8. oxygen
9. coxswain
10. boxing
11. antitoxin
12. equinox
13. oxcart
14. oxidation
15. oxygen mask

Just the Facts, page 37
1. four
2. disgusting little beast, filthy nuisance, miserable creature
3. Central Park
4. a. centipede
   b. grasshopper
   c. ladybug
   d. earthworm
   e. spider
5. earthworm
6. ten hairs
7. juice
8. Answers will vary.
9. rose, tummy
10. hole in the peach
11. bump

GA1459

Drills for Skills, page 39

1. kiwi $2/4 = 1/2$
2. peeve $3/5$
3. skiing $2/6 = 1/3$
4. bazaar $3/6 = 1/2$
5. revere $3/6 = 1/2$
6. solo/Oslo $2/4 = 1/2$
7. caravan $3/7$
8. evergreen $4/9$
9. onto $2/4 = 1/2$
10. Alaska $3/6 = 1/2$
11. infinity $3/8$
12. murmur $2/6 = 1/3$
13. lava $2/4 = 1/2$
14. unduly $2/6 = 1/3$
15. tumult $2/6 = 1/3$

Vexing Vocabulary, page 40

1. game
2. blame
3. dame
4. flame
5. fame
6. America
7. lame
8. same

1. breach
2. reach
3. beach
4. bleach
5. preach
6. teacher
7. peach
8. each other

Just the Facts, page 52

1. motto for all witches
2. Norwegian
3. head
4. chocolate
5. police chief of Norway
6. Solveg disappearing into a painting
7. Royal Society for the Prevention of Cruelty to Children
8. hotel manager
9. one hundred
10. addresses; summon, contact
11. Norway
12. 500, 500
13. fruit bowl, four
14. Magnificent, Bournemouth
15. William and Mary
16. maximum

Drills for Skills, page 55

1. Baa, baa, black sheep, Have you any wool?
2. God bless America, land that I love
3. There was an old woman who lived in a shoe
4. Hey diddle diddle, The cat and the fiddle
5. Old King Cole Was a merry old soul
6. Pease porridge hot, Pease porridge cold Pease porridge in the pot
7. Little Miss Muffet Sat on a tuffet Eating her curds and whey

Jack and Jill went up the hill

Mary had a little lamb, Its fleece was white as snow

Rock-a-bye baby in the treetop

Jack Sprat could eat no fat, His wife could eat no lean

Georgie Porgie pudding and pie, Kissed the girls and made them cry

Hickory, dickory, dock, The mouse ran up the clock.

Humpty Dumpty sat on a wall, Humpty Dumpty had a great fall

Short-Term Project, page 57

1. stop
2. hurry
3. help
4. sold
5. think

GA1459

Drills for Skills, page 69

1. twins
2. between
3. twigs
4. twelve
5. twice
6. twine
7. Hotwax
8. Antwerp
9. twinkle
10. tweet
11. Mark Twain
12. twist
13. tweezer
14. outward
15. twirl
16. twilight
17. tweed
18. twitch

Just the Facts, page 80

1. Imhrat Khan
2. 41, single
3. London, West Indies, France
4. Ferrari™
5. France, England, United States
6. administrator
7. a policeman
8. orphanages S.A.
9. system
10. fire walking
11. swift, sudden
12. levitation
13. threading a needle
14. exercise book
15. canasta

Just the Facts, page 96

1. F
2. F
3. F
4. F
5. F
6. F
7. T
8. T
9. F
10. F
11. T, F
12. F
13. F
14. F
15. F

Just the Facts, page 110

1. *Easy Cooking*
2. hair
3. with sawdust in oil
4. *Great Expectations*
5. green
6. times
7. threw her over the fence
8. newt
9. Lavender
10. turned over a glass
11. car
12. precocious
13. purple
14. Spain
15. Miss Honey
16. plane

Short-Term Project I, page 116

I.
1. 5221
2. 7863
3. 447
4. 757
5. 6663
6. 255
7. 694
8. 105
9. 5030
10. 565

II.
a. to
b. at
c. pun
d. ad
e. in
f. ore
g. van
h. pot
i. ale
j. us (09)

III.
1. nips–4779
2. oven–1993
3. sled–6898
4. Ken–393
5. aves–3999
6. eves–9999

IV.
I'd–38; can't–8255; I'll–721

V.
open–1193
Answers will vary.

VI.
Answers will vary.

Just the Facts, page 126

1. India
2. toothpaste factory
3. the grandparents and their bed
4. eatable, lickable
5. balmy   daffy
   nutty   goofy
   screwy   beany
   batty   buggy
   dippy   wacky
   doty   loony
6. Viking boat of old
7. Mike Teavee
   Charlie Bucket
   Augustus Gloop
   Veruca Salt
   Violet Beauregarde
8. ten
9. Nutty Crunch Surprise
10. $500
11. Veruca
12. pink
13. Mrs. Salt
14. five seconds
15. Willy's lake
16. eating
17. pieces

Just the Facts, page 139

1. driftwood
2. camera
3. eight or nine
4. distance from Jamaica to the Eleuthera Island in miles
5. wandered off lost, kidnapped
6. turtle soup, steak, shell souvenir
7. doornail
8. speaker doesn't know
9. frightful
10. mammoth

GA1459

Drills for Skills, page 142

1. red   redo
2. pint   pinto
3. cell   cello
4. bo   boo
5. to   too
6. Tang™   tango
7. ore   Oreo™
8. bing   bingo
9. ring   Ringo
10. lass   lasso
11. gall   Gallo
12. ole   oleo
13. burr   burro

Short-Term Project, page 144

Clock I

1. plain
2. rap
3. bait
4. game
5. sag
6. rate
7. nap
8. bag
9. plate

Clock II

1. plant
2. hand
3. tank
4. sang
5. band
6. mane
7. rant
8. Hank
9. sane

GA1459